Be Alarmed!

The Hostile Effects of Capitalism and Democracy

ALEXANDER "ELIAZAR" NAWLS

ISBN 978-1-63885-367-1 (Paperback)
ISBN 978-1-63885-368-8 (Digital)

Covenant Books, Inc.
11661 Hwy 707
Murrells Inlet, SC 29576
www.covenantbooks.com

Preface

The hostile effects of capitalism and democracy breeds chaos in America and abroad. This system, like most other systems of government, was devised by man. Democracy, socialism, communism, and autocracy merely effectuate the designs and will of men. Capitalism as a system of Governance breeds insatiable greed, and moral depravity. Any governmental system absent the fear of God past and present has been proven to be systematic failures to their respective societies. They become intrusive, blinding, and psychologically numbing as to their harsh realities and physical effects. Through this book, I have labored to give a meticulous display of the aforementioned effects in perspective. For the record, it behooves all humanity to be advised. God puts men in power over nations, and their ill will that is contrary to God's will does not go unchecked by divine intervention.

Introduction

"Woe is me. Woe is me," cries the earth shrouded with a hazardously polluted environment. Earth, the facilitating matrix for the reproduction and sustainment of life, is now ailing as a result of man's greed and ignorant designs. Today's stewards of the earth have proven themselves unworthy of God's prime directive respective to our domain. The chief stewards of the earth are known predominately by their reckless stewardship of the earth and boisterous claims of being superpowers. They all have their respective gods and ideologies; nevertheless, as leaders of the world, they've become exceedingly disoriented. The Lord God, by most holy decree, directed man and gave him dominion over the earth. As biblically inscribed in Genesis: 1:27–28, God created humans and empowered them to be fruitful, to multiply, and to replenish the earth. Yes, ultimately, the Lord directed man to subdue the earth. Unarguably, to have dominion is to have stewardship requiring planetary and environmental considerations effectuated through our responsibilities and deeds as humans. However, in the absence of good virtue, the disorientation of nations is a result of being religiously disingenuous, thus deteriorating morally and psychologically to a state of ungodliness and truculence.

CHAPTER 1

War and Death

By illuminating the hostile effects of capitalism and democracy on the world and humanity at large, I am sounding a moral alarm. America in her pride has boasted profusely of her power and greatness throughout the world. People in general are of like manner: in awe of greatness and humbled by or attentive to power. Let us now reflect on America's less than humble beginnings. History has portrayed the American immigrants as what could be construed as exiles.

These exiled immigrants I perceived to be predominantly misfits of a society dominated by elitists. England, former homeland to the immigrants, banished them in an effort to rid themselves of a loathsome burden. History further reveals the American immigrants as being referred to as the scum of England. This referral at its very least calls into question the very core of their predominate character. At this time, I direct your attention to what I perceived as inevitably preordained events. The intransigent immigrants embarked on the shores of what ultimately became America. The exiled immigrants predestined in their quest to conquer the land cunning and seductively alluring. They ultimately seized upon the near-primitive native Indians.

The American immigrants arrived here idealistically in pursuit of a new homeland. Upon arrival, the natives greeted them with unsuspecting benevolence. The natives, primitive in their means, taught the immigrants to survive in the so-called New World. With commitment to intent and purpose, the immigrants maintained a fixed perspective on their goal. The immigrants, it seemed, were intent on acquiring the land by any means necessary. In the quest to achieve their goal, the immigrants employed the use of what I perceived as germ warfare in the use of disease-laden blankets, most indefensible aligned with other advanced stratagems of war against the natives. The immigrants launched a succession of tactical subversions on the natives witfully unmatched. The natives, in a near-primitive stage of intellectualism, subsequently as a result of subversion, nary affliction was put on notice. Being apprised of the immigrant's egregious offenses, the natives began to unite in defensive posture. This to the immigrants was no doubt perceived as retaliatory; thus, the hostilities soared, and ultimately war ensued. As a result of the aforementioned events regarding the life and times of the early immigrants, a new nation was formed at the cost of very near annihilation of another race.

However unfortunate the aforementioned events of the past are, the immigrants had achieved their goal. The immigrants, victorious in their quest to obtain the land, gave birth to what ultimately became America. As the author of this book, I endeavor to make clear that war and slavery were the sowing of the seeds of capitalism and democracy. Through a meticulous display of the contents of this book on the past- and present-day life, I endeavor to make plain the hostile effects of capitalism and democracy at large. The birth of this American system of capitalism and democracy ostensibly gave way to a righteous and wholesome way of life. While I am an American citizen assimilated, born, and raised, I am grateful but nonetheless grieved by the destructive means of our emergence. It is my personal opinion that the events of life today are the promises of life tomorrow. Thus, I submit to you my goal in the writing of this book: It is to elicit a rational sense of alarm in the American citizenry. For the record, I'm proposing we display the type of alarm that compels us to speak out and seize to acquiesce to the country's destructive path in life to date.

I would certainly be remiss were I not to make mention of the goodness that is in part America. Over time, America has made great strides in progress as a country. Capitalism and democracy have been the gateway to advancement by way of capital and freedom. America has amassed a wealth of life-sustaining support systems through technology, science, research, production, and distribution. This system of capitalism and democracy has been the beating heart of the American people's endeavors at large. As all things worth having in life comes with a price, it's this system that has provided our most valued necessities that enable us to have our vast spectrum of life, a quality of life that is often taken for granted. This system has notably provided our security, freedom, the right to choose, and for some, the complete benefit of the Constitution. All this is, in part, America and her self-imposed limited potential. Why limited potential, you ask. This question and an array of others will be answered throughout this book.

Definitively, capitalism is an economic system in which the means of production and distribution are privately owned and operated for private profit. This system, when utilized honestly for all intents and purposes, is logical and extremely productive. Capitalism in my opinion requires three necessary components vital to its overall use and success. Democracy is the critical component of the capitalistic system. Democracy is denoted as a system of government in which all the people share political control. However, neither can be successful without justice by way of balance. Capitalism, democracy, and justice are inseparable for continued success in a system of governing.

However, honesty and integrity are essential for greater life expectancy of such a system of governance. Honesty and integrity are in essence the foundation of good character. America to date has not fared well for such esteemed virtues. In my opinion, America has been plagued with war and death as a result of her ill deeds at home and abroad. In her beginning, the American immigrants made strategic use of the principles of capitalism at war to secure the country. With elevated tactics of cruelty beyond belief for the natives, the immigrants methodically capitalized on the weaknesses of the native Indians.

America, at this point, was no doubt proud of her valiant efforts and full of herself. The citizenry began to experience a new and lavish sense of freedom: Americans having only to stake a claim to a patch of land could build their homes. They began the common nurturance of life—tilling the soil, planting, and raising livestock. While this ostensibly has the glow of a beautiful life, clearly the opposite rings true, bearing in mind that these were at this point the descendants of the exiled and otherwise voluntary immigrants of England.

History oddly enough foretold of the predominant character of the immigrants when they were referred to as the scum of England. In the early stages of an apparent forced migration, historically, the reality of the immigrants' character and lifestyles were embellished and camouflaged over time. When the immigrants are referred to as pioneers and revolutionists, the realities can be misconstrued or bloated. These terms give a boastful air to what is in reality at the very least a farce. Having been banished from their homeland, they had become what is today termed exiles. When realities are unmasked, it makes obvious the fact that the predominate portion of exiled immigrants had very little to pass on by way of virtues. Some, however, were obviously educated and maintained the character and sheer grit it took to get across the ocean. While labeled the scum of

England, some of the immigrants had been upstanding citizens made enemies of the state, expelled from Europe for speaking their mind against the monarchy, also known as righteousness.

In time, I surmise, the immigrants became weary faced with what was obviously a mind-boggling and daunting task of nation-building. Somewhere in the deep, dark crevices of a heathenish mind, the idea of slavery was conceived. This, in my opinion, would be the second display of the hostile effects of capitalism and democracy with the first being having capitalized on the weaknesses of the American natives. Effectively, the second display of capitalism and democracy in its entirety would be the capture or purchase and enslavement of blacks clearly for the capitalization of free labor. With this being said, the idea of slavery evolved to a grim reality.

These events, in my opinion, were the beginning stages of the ill will of capitalism and democracy. America it seems has always suffered a proportional divide ideologically. This divide over time manifested what is today known as the two ruling parties of government, the one being the Republicans and the other initiated the Democrats. This ideological divide I perceived as being the cause of the next phase of the hostile effects of capitalism and democracy. Over time, the war of the North and South ensued, induced in my view by a grievous dichotomy regarding slavery. The sad and morbid irony here is, a budding nation would undergo a war among themselves over the evil concept of slavery. Thus, I submit that this system of capitalism and democracy poorly regulated breeds the evils of greed, war, death, poverty, and moral deficiency and the deterioration of human virtue. If one tries to ascertain the amount of deaths that could be reasonably attributed to capitalism, the results would be frightening. When you examine the systemic attributes of capitalism and democracy, you'll find that money and power are its chief assets. It's a known fact in the world that power corrupts, and money is quite often at the root of all evil. For an immeasurable account of deaths induced by capitalistic greed categorically overtime, I ask your indulgence.

Deaths Spun by Way of Capitalistic Greed

Death due to war and slavery for profit.

Death due to cigarette sales for profit.

Death due to pharmaceutical companies' greed for profit.

Death due to unaffordable health care and manufactured poverty for profit.

Death due to corporations' insatiable greed and destructive practices for profit.

Death due to legal and illegal guns and drug sales for profit.

Death due to greed, stress, and the perils of life spun by capitalism for profit.

Death due to the poor regulation of hazardous products for profit.

Death due to a capitalistic government's insensitivity to war-torn military veterans.

Death due to obesity spun by failed FDA regulatory restraints and the adherence to comprehensive science. Indeed, the obsessive, beguiling, and possessive forces of capitalism are corruptive and compelling. Capitalism and democracy; are a system of governance while blinding, morally corruptive, obsessive and desensitizing, it's the system that guides the American way of life.

While I'm aware the system has worked in the past, I fear America is presently in denial or blissfully ignorant about our own state of affairs. This system of governance has gone from one that serves the public to one that is served by the public. Our government is presently indebted to foreign governments for trillions of dollars, to my complete dismay. We've been engaged in wars that are costing billions of dollars; these wars and rumors of war have been ongoing for years with no real end in sight. The government to date has been incapable of giving a justifiable explanation for the Iraq War initial lunge respective to the American public. In early 2007, the former president George W. Bush announced an unspecified budget upward of a trillion dollars largely in support of the war effort. We, the American people, had lost over ten thousand in military personnel; the Iraqi people had lost some thirty-four thousand civilians in a report by the ABC News late 2006 to 2007. Our government talked of Iraq's desire to have a democracy and the importance of an American victory in the war. Ironically, for a war without reason, we hoped for victory, spent money we didn't have, and sacrificed our people.

To America, I pose these questions.

- When did we acquire such an affection for Iraq?
- Was it worth the price and sacrifice?
- What will be the face of victory in the ongoing wars?
- What will be the extenuating consequences of the wars in Iraq and abroad?

In America, our present system of governance, capitalism and democracy, is failing the American public. How then do we make it work abroad? Today, America weighs her options for an exit strategy to the extended wars that have become an imbroglio of grief, death, and destruction for America and, proportionally, the world. In contemplation of an exit strategy for the present theater of war, America is wearied with new wars and the threat of war looming on the horizon. We, the commoners of America, sit quietly, wondering how it all came about.

While very few are privy to the decision-making of the executive inner circle of our government, I could only speculate on the reasons for the war's initial launch to have been twofold. With respect to reasons, one was personal in nature, speculatively, which I won't elaborate; and the second, while imperiously totalitarian, I suspect it was a sheer display of the ill will of American capitalism at play. First off, I ask your indulgence for my theoretical perspective initially. When we examine the prospects of oil being a motive for the present war's initial launch, it lends credence to the following perspective: One could perceive, as I have, the Bush and Cheney administration's personal business holdings in oil as having been a conflict of interest for American governance. With this administration's inability to give a reasonable justification for the Iraq War, this perspective was enhanced speculatively. Furthermore, the George W. Bush administration, to the complete dismay of some, had been slow or unwilling to fund alternative fuel resources appropriately. The demand for oil across the globe escalated; as a result, the prices skyrocketed. This scenario no doubt presented vast opportunities for oil barons and affiliated associates. Due to the overall scenario, the American citizenry has suffered exhaustively. In light of this perplexing imbroglio, the ludicrous effects of that administration's policies continued.

As previously mentioned, our government had proposed a new budget proposal for upward of a trillion dollars. As usual, the arguments by way of reasoning were in support of our vital interest regarding the war. If this war was indeed in the vital interest of America, why wasn't the draft initiated? It seems the multiple tours of duty by our service personnel not only warranted such actions but also required it. The failure of Bush's two administrations to initiate the draft and the US Senate's unwillingness to demand it was suspect in my view. It seemed this war was being fought with a devious air of social preference.

This volunteer military consists for the most part of kids of the less fortunate. In today's military, kids are lured by offers of resources or opportunities otherwise unaffordable or obtainable.

The question I've posed is, would the war have been fought differently with the draft initiated? My point in fact is, with the draft initiated, the more affluent would experience more severely the woes of this war. Our government has expressed gratitude, sorrow, and regret for the sacrifice, loss of lives, and otherwise horrid effects of the war; however, it is entirely different when the loss is one of your own. In the absence of a justifiable explanation for the war, our motives were at best suspect at home and abroad. The war efforts have been a travesty regarding loss of lives and resources to date, and I fear there will be no success worthy of our sacrifices.

Initially, the war in my opinion had all the trimmings of an elaborate deceit. Notably, it has been said that the truth in the dark will soon come to light. If this war was in fact a result of the ill will of capitalism for oil or the weapons manufacturing industry, it will come to be known as such. When you have observed and accessed the big picture regarding the war, you begin to wonder, why were we in Iraq? If we were there merely in pursuit of a few thugs, aka terrorists, at a cost of billions, I submit to you that the intellectual prowess of some in government is failing us egregiously.

Outside of securing the oil reserves of imperialistic designs, nothing else seemed feasible. Be that as it may, the war has expanded and continues to drain America, a nation in peril. Thus, I submit to the American public it's for these reasons and the like that we must display a rational sense of alarm. For too long, the needs of the American public have been shamelessly neglected or piecemealed at best; as a result, the economic engine of capitalism and democracy has been denatured. This system that is now malfunctioning impacted and stagnated with the selfish designs of those empowered is failing us.

Our system of capitalism and democracy has outgrown its infrastructure, bloated with greed and thievery of corporate thugs and the like. The system is now critically hemorrhaging resources through infractions of poor governance. Thus, I implore the American public to cease and desist with the simple acquiescence of failing politics and procedures. Americans must begin to deploy the full brunt of democratic empowerment to alert the helm. It is time to plot a new course. The American people are frustrated, and some have begun to vent irrationally. Oprah Winfrey was recently criticized for her humanitarian efforts in Africa. By donating a school, Oprah was graciously planting a seed of hope in the fertile soil of tomorrow in a land near hopelessness.

Oprah Winfrey, Bill Gates, Tyler Perry, and others are monumental icons of hope and champions for the plight of others. While acknowledging that they are enormously blessed in life, one should note that it is not the responsibility of any individual to shoulder America's burdens. The American people at large are frustrated and in need of help. Our two-party system of government of late seems to take us one step forward and two steps back. At one point, the Clinton administration had amassed an economic surplus. Its successor, the George W. Bush administration, succeeded in accumulating a deficit figuratively, which is inconceivable to most Americans. This fluctuation of our economic state offers very little hope for the future.

When we look honestly at the status of American life today, it is clear America is self-destructing. Our system of capitalism and democracy has indeed become hostile to the public. It's a well-known fact that strong nations are comprised of strong families. Proportionally, government and our elite citizenry seem to turn a blind eye to the ailing public. Put bluntly, America needs to reassess her complete modus operandi. America, home of the brave and land of the free, is fast becoming a land of despair. The disparity in my opinion is due to a lack of leadership and unwillingness to reinvest in ourselves. Our people are suffering and dying on too many fronts for no good reason; for the record, premature and untimely deaths limit America's potential. Clearly there needs to be more emphasis put on sensitivity, compassion, and intellectual capabilities of those seeking the capacity of governance.

In my opinion, the office of the president must step up its performance in making critical results-yielding decisions. The decisions regarding the critical issues of today must be groundbreaking, yielding results in a critical-needs time frame. An empire most often collapses from within; thus, it is essential that America focuses on the needs of her premier capital, which I deem to be the American citizenry. Nearing the end of this chapter, I feel it is necessary to reiterate my call for alarm. I simply ask that we be true to ourselves. As stated, our people are dying at an alarming rate, and prosperity is on the decline. Until recently, the government seemed uncertain of the future or at the very least unwilling to acknowledge our frailties.

Our two-party system of governance is too often stagnated by their inability to agree. Their constant engagement of logorrhea gives a real sense of how out of touch some in our government truly are. What does it say about us when we have to have a House senatorial debate in the medical cases in support of our wounded troops? For far too long, America has been unwilling to invest wisely on health care, education, and gainful employment ventures for the mass public. There is an unfair distribution of wealth plaguing America and stalling the great engine of capitalism. As I see it, our system of government requires a principled sense of economic balance to work successfully.

If America is to survive and maintain her status as the world leader, we must conclude the present war responses to date as sufficient to pull out. Our government must assess the legitimate needs of our society and plot a course of success. We must better regulate corporations and government policies to support and suffice the needs and overall well-being of the country. Business elites must cease with the every man for himself mentality. In essence, America must pool her resources to generously strive to rebuild, restrengthen, and reassert ourselves competitively at home and abroad. Ultimately, we must do away with selfish greed and insensitivity toward our own. Perhaps we have lost sight of what is important in a person-to-person relationship as human beings. Nevertheless, we must concede that everyone's peace and prosperity hinges on our sense of value for one another and our embrace of the true and living God.

Today, our troops depend on one another at war on a campaign to achieve the obscure goals of our government. Tomorrow, our youth will be depended upon to hold the line and maintain the American way of life. Thus, it's incumbent upon those empowered to govern that they strategically provide for the future. While we can appreciate the economic wizardry of some of our profound economists, forecasts and realities fall short. I have observed this for some time, and I've concluded the fault lies with our executive branches of government. The mounting deaths of our troops abroad and untimely deaths at home due to lagging health care are a testament to failed policies, mismanagement, and the obtuse faculties of some in government. America's system of capitalism democracy is on a downhill spiral and cannot continue to go unchecked. It has presently become a vicious cycle with an influx of greed, crime, poverty, and psychological despair. Thus, I submit to concerned members of the government and society at large that we must display alarm and elicit change.

CHAPTER 2

Social/Psychological Engineering

Bear with me as I give my perspective on one of the most despicable crimes against humanity induced, I fear, by capitalistic greed. By general consensus, money is by and large found to be at the root of all evil. As previously depicted, capitalism is an obsessive, beguiling, and possessive force that often employs deception to meet one's desired objective. When I examine the use of cow's milk and concocted formulas for the nourishment of human infants, I'm puzzled, to say the least. Personally, I've often wondered how it all came about. I've looked at the world with stifling wonderment as to why no one questioned such a denaturalizing altering of humanity.

As I observed other forms of life, they all seem to follow age-old mannerisms. Early on in life, I began questioning adults as to why they used canned milk as opposed to breast milk for infants. It seemed odd that when questioning men and women, they all gave inadequate or intellectually insufficient responses. Men gave haphazard responses, like it's cheap or it's convenient. When I asked women, they seemed puzzled or slightly irritated, uttering things like breastfeeding is embarrassing, it hurts, or something to the tune of being socially inappropriate. As time went on, I recall media displays of new and improved formulas for infants. Being a layperson, I could only conclude that cow's milk and formulas lacked the necessary nutrients to precisely fortify infants. I continued to pay attention as manufacturers continued to produce diverse formulas. While it's never been said this adventure was formed out of capitalistic greed, I suspected no less.

As time went on, physicians found they had to assess and prescribe formulas to meet the individual needs of infants. Obviously, nothing could be more important for infants than milk for nutrition by oral consumption. However, it seemed their new formulas had compounding problems in areas of processing and medical assessments of side effects. Having taken the aforementioned issues into account, I was even more puzzled as to why society at large would pursue such a perplexing and problematic altering of humanity.

Over time, I had vigorously pondered this issue to the point of weariness. It was inconceivable to me that science and the medical community had not perceived early on that cow's milk and concocted formulas were nutritionally inadequate. By a brief process of elimination, it seemed so elementary to assess the wide range of required nutritional differences of needs between cattle and humans. Let's face it, the source of cow's nourishment and humans are vastly different. For me, this issue had become a perplexing imbroglio of confusion and utter dismay. At this point, I began to suspect the motives of those in power. I had to have closure. When I looked at the bigger picture, this was more than a simple change of the nutritional source for infants; this was a change of epic proportion. This change brought on the altering of humanity, human health deterioration, and a vast new market of consumer goods facilitating the emergence of a robust financial conglomerate. After weighing the aforementioned events, I began to come categorically to terms with the basis of what I perceived to be moral depravity at play. Obviously, this complete concept and radical altering of humanity ratiocinated from a flawed premise.

When examining realistically the theory of the mass substitution of breastfeeding, there were numerous red flags. There is in fact a preponderance of scientific evidence past and present indicating cow's milk and formulas as insufficient for the nourishment of human infants. It's been said all things, to some extent, are comprised of a chemically based complex. With this as a premise, I would think it scientifically comprehensible for a human's chemical complex respective to a mother's milk being spiritually measured. It's nutritionally incomparable. Based on pure logic alone, I would venture to say that insufficient nourishment for humans at such an early stage in life would be conducive to bad health. While I'm not a scientist or a chemist, I simply doubt man's ability to match God's delicate balance of the superior in-depth functions and needs of an infant's individual needs.

With feeding being the primary purpose for a woman's breast, I doubt there can be any rational justification for the mass substitution of breastfeeding. Moreover, I pose this question: What motivated this unconscionable altering of humanity? Women are generally born with two breasts and physically capable of nourishing their infants. Absent physical ailments or deficiencies, a mother's milk is the most nutritionally fortifying nourishment for human infants. Manufacturers in conjunction with science powered by the insatiable greed of corporations have continually tried unsuccessfully to enhance cow's milk and formulas as an efficient substitute for breast milk. However, this process has been plagued with inefficiencies and harmful effects often reported but camouflaged.

In the use of cow's milk for infants, some of the early indications of its inadequacies were in preparation. In effect, a cow's milk has to undergo an array of procedural processes for human consumption. Unlike the milk of a woman, cow's milk is externally pasteurized and homogenized. Absent a real interest in this process, these terms can be definitively obscuring. Understandably, we are laypeople to the terms of this process; thus, I've labored to make things plain definitively in summary.

Pasteurization. This is the process of controlled heating of milk to destroy bacteria and arrest spoilage without affecting flavor (Louis Pasteur, 822–95, French chemist).

Homogenization. This is the process of making milk more uniform by the emulsification of its butter fat (i.e., refined).

While these are but two basic steps for milk processing, the inefficiencies are ongoing. When we investigate milk's overall process, there are diverse phases and additives to cow's milk and an array of chemical treatments to dairy cattle. I won't bore you with the complete details of the processing of cow's milk for the following reasons: It's unnecessary, hazardous, and one of the key enterprises of the hostile effects of capitalism and democracy. For further information on cow's milk and its process and harmful effects, see the reference portion of this book.

I posed a question early on in this chapter: What motivated this unconscionable altering of humanity? Well, I submit to you that money is in fact at the root of this unconscionable act. The MCGA dairy industry past and present continues to spend billions of dollars to glamorize the drinking of cow's milk and to convince us it's nutritionally wholesome and sufficient. Any and all such statements are camouflaging fabrications and propaganda to brainwash society at large for the financial gain of this industry. There is in fact scientific evidence and claims to the contrary (see "Milk—The Hidden Toxins" http://www.antidairycoalition.com.)

Adverse Health Effects
American Family Physicians, September 15, 2001
"Promoting and Supporting Breastfeeding"

Dr. David Meyers, MD, Georgetown University
School of Medicine, Washington, DC

Family physicians, as doctors of women and children, are in the ideal position to promote and support breastfeeding. The American Academy of Family Physicians (AAFP) has the following policy: "Breastfeeding and infant nutrition" states that "human milk is the optimal form of nutrition for infants." With input from AAFP, the US Department of Health and Human Services has published "Breastfeeding: HHS Blueprint for Action on Breastfeeding," an up-to-date, comprehensive review of the evidence of the medical and economic benefits of breastfeeding for women, children, families, and employers.

David Meyers, MD, in the recent past, completed a fellowship in health policy and research in the Georgetown University School of Medicine Department of Family Medicine and is a member of the American Academy of Family Physicians advisory committee on breastfeeding.

Contrary to what societal elites promote and fabricate as truth and advancement for the human health of the so-called modern world, the negative effects of cow's milk and concocted formulas outweigh the positive effects as a substitute for breastfeeding. The mass substitution of breastfeeding in effect constitutes a condescending exploit from superior idealism for that of an inferior design and prospect.

In a world reeling from an onslaught of old and new diseases and human health incursions, mainstream society maintains a flawed perspective and fixation with the denaturalizing custom of the mass substitution of breastfeeding. Many of our societal elites of the health and dairy industry continue to promote and offer the psychologically subversive concept of choice as it relates to breastfeeding. This, in my humble opinion, is outrageous idealistically as it misleads and subjects the mass public to the hidden toxins and adverse health effects of growth hormones and added chemicals injected into cows to increase the production of milk.

Social/psychological engineering is a captivating web spun by the psychologically possessed humans likened to the arachnids. Metaphorically speaking, some humans are like a rare breed of the most treacherous spiders, weaving a contriving web infecting mass society with deceptive venom. While speaking metaphorically, the realities are grim as it relates to the alluring tactics deployed to prey on the masses for financial gain. Cow's milk and an array of concocted formulas are well-camouflaged in respect to the untold detriment of their human health hazards.

In what could be construed as a rebirth of moral consciousness and astounding intellectualism, some in the medical profession are beginning to abandon the flawed perspective of the mass substitution of breastfeeding. I would surely be remiss were I not to voice my opinion in depth for how and why this perplexing imbroglio came about.

As to the question of how and why this demonic exploitation of humanity was hatched, one has to acknowledge that spiritual disorientation is an invitation for evil. In my opinion, this force of evil is in effect a substantial form of an intrinsically tactical force deployed by Lucifer, otherwise known as Satan. The aforementioned force to the spiritually inclined is biblically denoted as temptation. Being spiritually disoriented renders us humans vulnerable to a state of boundlessness to the seductive temptations of Satan. With the state of America and the world being as such as it is, this perspective is given credibility. While it's true, human and spiritual disorientation is nothing new. The mass substitution of breastfeeding, like other forms of human perversion, provokes the wrath of God. When we take into account the mounting deaths of women attributed to breast cancer, I suspect and categorize this as a plague, in biblical terms, signaling God's heated displeasure with one of humanity's most odious acts of human perversion.

Early on, I referred to the mass substitution of breastfeeding as a crime against humanity. Bear with me while I elaborate on this point to further illuminate the depth of this unconscionable connivance of evil for profit. This obstructionist act plays to the very core of what I perceive as the hostile effect of capitalism and democracy.

This evil act of connivance was orchestrated by some of the leading minds of science, research, medicine, and financial financiers. With this formidable group of intellects aligned, one would assume it elementary to have anticipated the potentially harmful effects of the mass substitution of breastfeeding as the most lucid. When we assess this endeavor through a process of intellectual deductions, the nutritional food source of cows produce adequately for the complex physiological needs necessary for a cow's physical makeup, life, and the profundity of its reproductive capability. This logic requires no stretch of imagination. In the context of feasibility, I would think it logical that the aforementioned perspective would be applicable similarly for the physiological functions of humanity. For the record, I don't think it takes an intellectual phenomenon to concede this concept as intellectually feasible. While it is true the dairy industries and the manufacturers of infant formulas add vitamins and a host of substitutes aligned with an allotment of chemical inductions to cow's milk, the aforementioned products have consistently maintained levels of inadequacies and hazardous effects, thus proving to be incomparable to breast milk.

Medical researchers, to their credit, have continued to monitor the qualities and inequalities of cow's milk and concocted infant formulas over time. It's on behalf of what I perceive as an escalation of moral consciousness and due diligence in the advocacy and commitment to human health that I salute these vanguards of health care. I would surely be remiss were I not to acknowledge the various other frontliners and alarmists to the hazards of cow's milk and the effectual connivance of camouflaging fabrications and propaganda to brainwash society at large for financial gain. (For more information, see http://www.antidairy-coalition.com.)

Some in the medical community and others are striving to reinstate the common practice and natural way of humanity respective to the nurturance of human infants. The effects of the mass substitution of breastfeeding are catastrophic and warrants the reassessment of the federal government. Results of studies evaluating why American women choose not to breastfeed expose a relentless barrage of psychologically subversive tactics that include a lack of broad social/medical support for breastfeeding. It is for these reasons that I implore America and world leaders to cease and desist with the apostatizing of spiritual, moral, and principal virtues critical to the sustainment of humanity.

As I see it, the mass substitution of breastfeeding is an ill-conceived notion of an arrogant and ill-morale cultural diversion promulgated by the inspired evil intent to supersede or disregard the superior intellect of God. Thus, it's most logical for the United States to take the helms in the reversionary process as we are the most capable and resourceful for the task. Truthfully, I'm unclear if we (America) may or may not be responsible for the overall concept, but certainly, America is by and large responsible for its proliferation.

While I salute the current efforts of the medical community, I think a more aggressive approach is needed. I think there needs to be a more forthright and in depth conveyance of the negative effects of this heinous transgression of humanity's domain. In effect, our medical elite will have to come clean if we are to awaken the sleeping giant that is our government. Ultimately, mass society has to be made aware of the gravity and detriment of the substitution of breastfeeding. In the end, we all have a responsibility to act as vanguards of human health and well-being.

To the Daughters of Eve

I am appealing to women to become more actively engaged with the issue involving the substitution of breastfeeding. For the record, any woman specifically born as such qualifies as a daughter of Eve. My appeal is to women who, in effect, share dominion over the earth and the responsibilities of its cultivation. I make this appeal to women because it is quite often the woman that gives pause to men when we exceed the boundaries of rationalism in our deeds. Put bluntly, women predominantly have consistently taken or been given a back seat on this issue of the substitution of breastfeeding. There is no offense intended in my perspective of women on this issue. For the record, I feel women's intuition in perspective is needed to culminate a conclusion to this issue. The substitution of breastfeeding has in effect inverted the natural ways of women respectively to one of their greatest gifts and distinctive abilities.

The inversion of the nourishing of human infants was without question, in my estimation, a diabolical scheme for financial gain or at the very least a foolish endeavor. As a devastating altering of humanity in my view, I would surmise it dilutes the chemical complex in the infancy stages of the physiological process with long-term effects. It is for the aforementioned reason that I implore women of all races and nationalities to be alarmed. Furthermore, I feel it is incumbent upon women to cease and desist with the simple acquiescence of this evil process. Women must come to terms with the fact that this denaturalizing altering has subtly subverted their natural instincts in the cultivating nurturance of infants. In essence, women have inadvertently become accomplice in the perpetual perpetration of one of the most heinous crimes against humanity. For the record, I am not a medical professional; however, medical researchers and others have revealed the negative effects of the substitution of breastfeeding with cow's milk or concocted formulas as nutritionally deficient. At this inference, I submit to women of all walks of life. It is imperative that women engage this issue and ultimately return to the blatantly obvious human normative of breastfeeding.

As money is the root of all evil, so, too, is the denaturalizing altering of the substitution of breastfeeding similarly or indicatively. Simply put, expanding the mere concept of the substitution of breastfeeding worldwide was an ill-contrived concept, as I see it, in the evil lust for financial gain. Humbly, I submit to women the world over. Man has succeeded in bringing the world to the brink of destruction. Thus, I'm appealing to women, as the divine cofacilitators in the matrix of humanity, to ponder the work of man, subverting God's intent through the design of your souls. It is my hope that the women of the world acknowledge through intelligent deductions that reverting to breastfeeding as a human normative reflects righteousness spiritually and moral consciousness.

How do our government and other world leaders justify the acceptance of the mass substitution of human breastfeeding? I can only conclude their best argument to be one of convenience or social inappropriateness for the modern world. This being the argument or no, this heinous act is nothing short of a crime against humanity at large. I submit to the American public and the world over that this is a grave sin and blatant disregard for the divine intellect of our Creator. In my view, man has sought to improve on divinity and overstepped his God-given dominion. In an appeal to your personal sense of reasoning, I pose this question: What is more convenient and cost-efficient than a woman's ability to physically produce nourishment in the womb and after giving birth?

When we access the twisted concept of social inappropriateness, it would suggest indecency. This very notion is outrageous and deceptive and inadvertently attempts to discredit God's superior insight for creation. While I view this sinful act as a slight against the Lord, it is in fact a vicious attack on the health of humanity. We (the public) must awaken and assert ourselves to this aggressively pernicious force to human health. The dairy industry and associates continue to lead the masses like sheep to the slaughter as society at large remains in a state of docile contentment. In the face of countless instances of broken trust by the government's FDA and cooperate executives, the public is stuck in a state of subliminal submissiveness.

Being an American citizen, I'm dismayed by the mounting greed induced by capitalism and this democracy. Subjacent to my dismay; I find it ironic that the same system that built America has become our infirmity for self-destruction. Obviously, America has excelled and achieved immeasurable success as a country. The magnitude of success has exceedingly surpassed the hope of the Founding Fathers. As an American citizen, I feel I can and must speak bluntly as to the severity of what I perceive as character flaws. In real talk, I have to say some in corporate and other industries are mercilessly unscrupulous by measure of their designs.

We as a country witness our seniors, the sick, and the less fortunate cry out to no avail. When we assess the many burdens of life, they are generally financial. Our governmental leaders are often insensitive, unwilling, or wrongfully beholding to corporations and vast business entities. It's for these reasons I feel an urgent necessity to speak out. To the American citizens, I say be alarmed. For in a democracy, we share the benefits as well as the faults. America, be warned. We should be conscious as we go forward into the complexities of life in the future. It's been said that communication is the key to life. Thus, I advise we personally access the events that sustain our lives. As humans, we must be more God-conscious in meditation and effectuating the fear of God in all our endeavors. Furthermore, we must display alarm where or whenever necessary to the ill-conceived notions of man.

The practice of social/psychological engineering is used proportionally in advertising and mass media to assimilate and compel the public idealistically. This practice has been used to glamorize, camouflage, distort, compel, deceive, and subvert the mass public for capitalistic gain. This practice, in my view, is the most effective psychoactive science in the arsenal of big business for profit. While this practice was no doubt construed as a stroke of genius, I view it as a form of seductive venom utilized in the hostile effects of capitalism and democracy.

Social\Psychological engineering is used to foster or solicit sales fueling the economic engine of capitalism. This system proposed to inform, suffice, and cater to the needs and national interests of the American public we find has been highjacked literally. The system is now used to accommodate the insatiable greed of big businesses and fueling the obsessive goals of the elite. The practice of social/psychological engineering as a means for productivity has a regretful irony; it has done as much harm as good. The deceivingly tactical use of this practice is to employ the designs and obsessive desire of the often unscrupulous predators of business and government. This practice is the evil force and seductive venom utilized to effectuate the denaturalizing altering of the nourishing of human infants.

The same practice was exercised in the exploitation and sale of cigarettes. While health officials have decried smoking as lethal, smoking has and continues to be responsible for the death and deteriorating health of millions. Armed with the facts of the health hazards of smoking and the use of cow's milk and formulas, they are equally apprised of environmental hazards and our economic plight. Having said this, the American people and society at large has to acknowledge the negative potential of the beguiling nature of capitalism.

America is faced with an economic meltdown and what amounts to an imbroglio of circumstances with grave consequences. Proportionally, government and business leaders are beguiled and obsessed with the insatiable greed induced by capitalism. It appears they themselves have been psychologically subverted. If in fact our elitist power brokers have fallen victim to their own venom, it would account for our increasingly subsidiary state nationally. When assessed, greed is a possessive obsession, blinding and psychologically corruptive to mental faculties. When this theory is applied to corporate and government's elitists officials proportionally, it illuminates the fault of our economic decline.

Today, America's most critical resources, wealth and military might, are being absorbed in the excruciating efforts at war in the Middle East. The Arabs squabbled among themselves before America existed, and I doubt seriously if they'll ever submit or peacefully embrace American democracy. I'll say for the record, through psychological engineering, our fears were exploited to gain public support for the Iraq War. This was, in my opinion, another illustration of the ill will and apparent destructive tendencies of President George W. Bush's administration.

One of the latest and most financially lucrative exploits of psychological engineering is the promotion, sale, and services of cell phones. In America, our governmental parties clash over an array of issues daily. The executive branch proves themselves inimical at home and abroad. Government officials are lobbied daily by lobbyist of diverse interests—pharmaceutical, phone, farming, dairy, insurance, and numerous others.

These companies are in pursuit of expanding their opportunities ultimately to obtain larger shares of public revenue. In the case of the promotion of cell phones, the public is psychologically engineered to view the phone as a device that provides business conveniences, personal safety, emergency assistance, and the like. The public is later convinced of its potential to possibly save the lives of their kids or loved ones in potentially threatening circumstances. Today, the public views personal cell phones as an advantageous necessity for family, business, and pleasure. Through a form of tactically seductive psychological engineering sales, opportunities are expanded.

All parties involved in the business unite and seize upon opportunities offering deals to boost sales and heighten demand. Subsequently, a thriving business is accelerated into a maze of assorted dealers, creating a vast new financial conglomerate. The cell phone, like most new technology, is initially viewed as advancement in productivity for business or public use. While we may welcome new technology as progress, in many forms of technology, you will find it often eliminates jobs, impairs judgment, and creates costly expenditures. The creation of new technology, you'll find, most often benefits big businesses, subverting human virtues associated with gainful employment in the sustainment of life.

If America is to regain her social and economic prominence, a searching of the soul is crucial. Thus, it's critical that the elitists of business and government reassess their values. Big businesses and government must concede that capitalism has ironically become a national infirmity. America, I submit to you that our present war, arrogant displays, dictatorial policies, greed, and imperialist demeanor are grandiose illusions of self-destructive practices. It has become blatantly obvious that our national interests are secondary to the interests of big businesses and the obscure goals of American elites. Fraudulent practices are rampant to the extent that the lives of the American people are, on occasion, jeopardized for financial gain. The critical needs of our most vital services, such as the CDC and FDA, are underfunded and disregarded as seemingly trivial. What will it take to alarm the masses throughout America? The American government has shown itself as increasingly incapable of constructive governance. Once again, I submit to the American people that time is of the essence. We must display a rational sense of alarm when necessary.

CHAPTER 3

Moral Depravity and Ungodliness

When you consider our lifestyle in America, you'll find there are two sides categorically. One side is comprised of a societal lifestyle overwhelmed with the harsh burdens of American life. These burdens consist of the ordinary toils of provisional necessities, work, parenting, and the constant striving to maintain the accommodating necessities that sustain your life. This overwhelming portion of societal life is complex in the sense that we are constantly reaching, striving, and struggling unsuccessfully. Our lack of success is most often a result of the insatiable greed of the elite and possessed by the obsessive tendencies of capitalism. The opposite side of societal life is driven by an external force induced ironically by the same possessive and obsessive tendencies. These obsessive tendencies I've surmised to have been inspired by the obsessive compulsion of capitalism and the unbridled freedoms of democracy. The obsessive compulsion, in my unprofessional opinion, seems psychoactively conducive to a form of psychosis synonymous with elitism and exaggerated illusions of grandeur.

At this point, we will give the two sides of life commonly known in the following terms: the wealthy and the poor. The wealthy people of America are empowered similarly as some in government: They both shape and design the multifaceted parts of American lifestyles. America is known for her liberty, the liberty that provides for the types of freedoms that have in some respects made America great. Because America has excelled to greatness, it is not to say her system of governance is justifiable. While America has never claimed perfection, America advocates rules and judges by a legal system of jurisprudence.

Jurisprudence is a philosophy or science of law that is in effect a particular system or division of law. A form of law that is devised by man, as such, this system merely promotes the will of man. When the will of man is exalted absent the fear of God, it opens a Pandora's box of human ills. In America, a country of ill-measured freedoms, society proportionally tends to overreach in their liberties. The overreaching of liberties has contributed to crime, moral depravity, and an ungodly denaturalizing and altering of human mannerisms.

When our government and wealthy corporations commit criminal acts of deception, thievery, deporting jobs, price gouging, and gainful exploitation, it's not only criminal but also immoral. The aforementioned crimes are rampant, inimical, and indicative of the sins that have historically induced the divine intervention of God. At this inference, I feel I would be remiss were I not to mention that religious leaders act as if they are completely oblivious to the aforementioned events. While the hands of the religious community are not clean and in need of redemption and repentance, their intervention could serve to that end.

The wealthy elites of America demean and prey on the poor. This, in essence, speaks volumes to the psychological state predominately of American power brokers. When I hear journalists ask when corporate America will regain a conscience, this to me is very telling of some in the media who recognize the insatiable greed of the elites. However, they can't make the simple deductions as depicted in the preceding chapters. Capitalism is an obsessive, beguiling, and possessive force that transcends righteous principles, inducing moral depravity touching ungodliness.

Capitalism, as a practice in business, is not unlike the practice of a merchant. While I've heard it said, I've found it's true. It's hard for merchants to be honest. The practice of capitalism like that of a merchant is a lucrative craft. Capitalism characteristically employs deception, moral depravity, and the inducement of a predatory nature in its deployment. Corporate elites who prey on the less fortunate, the sick, and the elderly ultimately are oppressing the public. When you assess the use of capitalism as our system of means in America, you will find this to be a foregone conclusion. For capitalism's continued success, we must return to principles for the provision of restraint and limitations.

When we consider the inevitability of human nature, strict regulation and a change of policy respectively to lobbyist is critical in our capitalistic system. Proportionally, in government and predominately those in corporate America are perceived to be without a conscience. Capitalism's money-crazed merchants of this democracy are yielding their ungodly fruit of dishonor. With America literally on her knees in an effort for resurgence, who will carry the torch for democracy? America has pathologically disabled herself in the self-destruction of her economy and the bewilderment of the public. What goes on in the minds of our elitist power brokers? It seems they are so blinded by their insatiable greed that they can't see the damning effect of their transgressions and inimical offenses.

When ill-measured freedoms are unleashed in a country at the helm of the world, this creates problems of catastrophic proportions for the world over. Surely we've all heard it said, "Too much freedom brings chaos." America is presently in a state of chaos. The ill-measured freedoms of democracy are expanding abominably. Freedom of religion has induced something of a horse race for public revenue in support of the, quote, unquote, "needs of the church." With the perverse behavior of some in the religious communities, parishioners are beginning to wonder where to turn. People attend churches of all denominations for diverse reasons. Life is becoming increasingly more complex, and people are seeking religious counsel, guidance, and spiritual comfort. Sadly, some are driven to drinking, drugs, or worse in an effort to escape the grim realities of life in the world today.

Having said this, attending churches does very little if anything to change the increasingly harsh conditions of life or the world. While we may not want to accept it, it appears the world is under siege. The attendance in churches appears to have increased of late; this is no doubt in hopes of change. You attend church and pay your tithes, but the changes you see are not seemingly for that of personal prayer. I think it's time religious leaders take to the front lines on issues of health care, home foreclosures, and education in support of the ailing public. Presently, the most visible changes seen in churches are the quality of the pastor's wardrobe and cars and the magnitude of the churches. While it's not my intention to offend, I think it is time we broaden our horizons concerning the challenges of life and the realities of the world. Perhaps our pastors and their flock would be better served with a more in-depth study of prophecies.

Life in the world is presently in a very perplexing state due to the exalted will of man in the absence of fear of God. It's my opinion that if man indeed feared God, the grave conditions of the world could not exist. While I am concerned about the state of the world, my immediate attention focuses on the plight of America. The present state of America is daunting, to say the least. Today, America is falling, besieged by its corporations and elitist power brokers ostensibly the leading citizens of the country.

There is, it seems, an ever-increasing facet of issues plaguing the country that require the public's unification in a demonstration of alarm in protest. At present, only the will of a minority is expressed as representative of the country despite the supposed representation of Congress and Senate. I think it's time the public stands up and exercises their democratic right. It's timeout for half measures and fruitless talk. When we saw the level of arrogance displayed over the Iraq War by former president George W. Bush and the blatant disregard for the interest of the public and veterans, I was completely dismayed.

I have loved and respected women all my life and would support righteous causes on their behalf at a moment's notice. It's my opinion that women on the battlefield should be a last resort. Obviously, women are equally as competent and capable as men in most areas. I simply think it is less than honorable, undignified, and shameless their being present on the battlefield prior to the desperate conditions that might warrant such actions. With men at home and some 1.3 million in jail literally enslaved, we have women on the battlefield. America, I humbly submit something is wrong with this pitcher. I'm not a pessimistic person, but when you observe America and the world, there are more evil forces at work than good.

Just for the record, I am a pragmatic, God-fearing person. My intentions are to convey my concerns in the form of constructive criticism. My hopes are to elicit a rational albeit peaceful sense of public alarm and initiate change. As an American citizen, I feel it's illuminating, patriotic, and the right thing to do. On the other hand, I'm a realist. We live in a very complex society under democratic rule. Some of our politicians are uncouth, estranged, and bound in gridlock as a result of poor governance and insensibility for our national interest. I imagine it's a difficult feat for politicians to come out publically in support or opposition of complex issues to a predominately dual party society. Taking this into account the public sometimes, as in the past, has to employ the democratic process by an aggressive display of alarm.

When you consider certain issues in your personal and family life, you will find we deal with perplexing issues in a similar way as our politicians. Take for instance the issues of morality in our democracy as it relates to abortion, homosexuals, and transsexual individuals. Most people are quietly devastated dealing with these issues in their personal and family lives. You often find yourself straddling the fence psychologically with conflicting emotions, caught up in the midst of indecision of acceptance or rejection of a now estranged relationship. This is a situation where relatives and others unparty to it agonize over it privately.

This again is a situation that evolved from the exalted will of man out of the ill-measured freedoms of democracy. As previously stated, such ill-measured freedoms were in effect the opening of a Pandora's box of ills. I will state again for the record: If man feared God and obeyed his laws, statutes, commandments, issues of religion, immorality, and imperialism, then humanity's denaturalizing altering would be less challenging morally and psychologically. These are in fact the daunting perplexities of life that plague humanity absent the fear of God. The more man exerts his will on earth, the more self-destructive humanity becomes. This is more apparent today as the nations of the world are poised in a state of indecision and in the midst of war and suspense of the evil intent of surrounding nations.

The most dominant nations and ostensibly the most civilized are cordoned off with armaments poised while surreptitiously watching the others. Each nation is so entrenched in fear and distrust of the other that they effectuate their surveillance from the pits of the sea to the dark crevices of the universe. The cycle of fear is so overwhelming it now penetrates the womb of nations, causing the host citizenry to be suspects. The American government is so caught in an imbroglio of fear and self-destructive tendencies that they have begun to suspect and inspect the national public. In light of the maddening conditions worldwide, man respectively of nations continues to think they're on a constructive path for humanity.

This mind-set in biblical perspectives is denoted as a state of reprobation. Due to the arrogance and failure of present-day Gentile nations to submit to the fear of God irrespective of what they build and alliances formed, there will be no peaceful coexistence of today's nations and the societies thereof. Such events would be contrary to prophecy exalting man's will over God. Peace in the world today is contingent upon the fulfill-ment of biblical prophecy. A peaceful coexistence of world nations absent the fear of God is an illusionary concept within itself. The fear of God provides purpose for man, and the life of humanity without purpose would be mere existence and bla-tantly abstract. Thus, we could all be perceived as perpetuat-ing a worthless existence. Existence of man without purpose breeds discontent, giving way to a type of instability that breeds destruction.

To confirm this theory, I direct your attention to the pres-ent state of the world. The state of the world today is so volatile, hostile, and hazardous it's nearly incomprehensible. The most dominant nations of the world have even begun to plant their strategic defense mechanisms into the vast crevices of the uni-verse. Biblical prophecy, as I perceive it, foretold of man's "nest among the stars" with the spiritually inspired interpretation of nest being man's space station among the stars. The book of Obadiah foretold of the prophecy of God's intervention to stave off the ill will of man: "Though thou exalt thyself as the eagle, and though thou set thy nest among the stars, thence will I bring thee down, saith the Lord" (Obadiah 1:2–4).

Look briefly at the most troubling issues that are plaguing America and, thereby, the world at large. It's the current war and the unconscionable neglect and predatory abuses by business elites and politicians alike that are foremost. The hostile effects of our unscrupulous merchants of capitalism are having a drastic effect on the American public. Obviously, this is of very little concern to some of America's political elites that benefit through lobbyists. By the relentless tactics of deceit and thievery by some of our unconscionable elite, the public suffers at every turn as they endeavor to maintain life-sustaining necessities.

Humbly I submit to you the elite members of society. A nation consists of more than greed and nuclear missiles to thrive. Selfishness and insensitivity by government leaders promote rebellion and anarchy. The evil acts being perpetrated by some of America's elite and the state of the nation is a sign of indifference to righteousness and justice. Thus, I submit that the sincere acknowledgment and fear of God would provide the critically needed morale restraint and conscience that some of our elites are sorely lacking. The robbery of the poor brings the wrath of God, and there is no wisdom or understanding or counsel against the Lord.

America is morally deteriorating, and the psychological state of the public is becoming increasingly hostile toward one another. Schoolkids are turning to violence—shooting, killing, raping in fits of rage and moral depravity. Proportionally, America's adults are sadly responding similarly, resolving differences in a blaze of gunfire, savagely raping women, attacking service workers, and escalating armed robberies. Vicious attacks on fellow citizens are rampant.

The overwhelmed judicial system has responded with an unprecedented number of incarcerations surpassing two million. This inimical behavior on the part of the public is a travesty and is becoming prevalent nationally. While this form of behavior is not unlike that of foreign nations, this fact only illuminates the degenerative state of the world. The American government is presently baffled with what could only be construed as a self-destructing imbroglio of utter confusion. The mutating behavior and fallout of the degenerative state of society with criminals and humanity at large is an epidemic and, biblically termed, a plague. While this plague has all but silenced our behavioral psychologists, there are numerous other plagues mutating and pernicious, staggering the CDC (Centers for Disease Control and Prevention).

While I am normally confident in the abilities of our medical professionals, I sense the elements of divine intervention in effect. The will of man has been exalted and threatens inconceivable destruction. The knowledge and fear of the true and living God is not a valued perspective; however, I'm certain it will be demonstrated as the spiritually imposed limits, to the ill will of man.

Our lifestyles have in fact peaked at a grim point of ostensible surrealism. This is a state in my view where the surreal expressions of the unconscious mind become manifest through the conscious events of life. Unfortunately, the conscious events of life on a mass scale are more similar to a nightmare than our dreams. When we look at America and the world at large, it is a sociological disaster. While America seeks to standardize the world, morality is besieged, and socioeconomically, we are in ruins. While there appears to be some dignity and stability among the wealthy, thorough observations liken them proportionately to crabs in a barrel or predators at the very least.

It seems it's time for a reality check in America. America boasts of being leaders of the free world. In a society where the least fortunate are socially engineered into a web of poverty and destruction to serve and sustain the lifestyle of the affluent, it's a sociological travesty.

CHAPTER 4

Slavery and Imperialism

The concepts of slavery and imperialism are conceptually infectious plagues of the minds of predominately immoral societies. Biblical history reflects the subscribers of these demoralizing customs as power-crazed immoral societies. History further foretold of the ruinous collapse of such ill-nourished societies. Babylon, Rome, and Egypt conquered many nations, killing and enslaving the societies in their quest for imperialism. While these nations undoubtedly achieved imperial statues, the ill-nourishment of slavery and imperialist nations of biblical history reaped a godly intervention of karma, resulting in their ruin.

America's past participation in slavery and today's recycle/improvising of slavery through convicts, foreigners, and suppressed wages signals an alarm. Slavery for a prevailing portion of America, it seems, was psychologically infectious and subject to transmutation, as such revealing a subconscious predetermination for superiority by way of elitism. Over time, this infection evolves like a form of cancer spreading as elitism gives way to an insane craze for imperialism. Proportionally, the psychoactive effects of America's past and present deeds have formed a negative image and provoked hostilities internationally. Nationally, recycled slavery and imperialist aspirations are draining America, a country presently in peril.

The problems causing the most turmoil for America iron-ically are induced by the insatiable greed of the elite citizenry and our system of government. The systematic treachery and egotism induced surreptitiously by capitalism and our ailing democracy has caused wealthy America to plummet from an iconic state to proportionally systematic predators. For the record, this characterization is reflected in those of an elitist state of mind. It's most unfortunate that those most capable resourcefully are the most unwilling to champion the causes beneficial to our national interest.

Hence, the irony continues. America has led the world in the production of pollutants to the air, water, and all such envi-ronmental hazards but most unwilling to lead the world efforts for change. Some in American government have even displayed a lost sense of civility and compassion for their fellow citizen.

Strangely, some in government have evolved to outright warmongers with the audacity to crave for imperialism. They are drunk with pride and arrogance, insensitive to the needs of the American public, and emboldened by the country's wealth and armament. Our present economic decline and a barrage of assaults by way of the elements in catastrophically proportional disasters are indeed divine intervention. When you observe the nations of the world today, not one of them exhibits the capac-ity to change the self-destructive path of humanity. Out of con-cern for America, my homeland and home to millions, I appeal to those in power to deflate your eagles and heed your ways.

Great nations of the past displayed the same forms of arro-gance, doubt, and disbelief concerning divine intervention. Where are they today? The leading nations of today seem to bear a grievous sense of similarities. When you observe the lead-ing nations at large, you'll find them to be for the most part arrogant, disoriented, dictatorial imperialists. Religious or righteous principles are ostensibly embraced worldwide but unfortunately fail to impact humanity's deteriorating virtues.

The rights and lives of the less fortunate are being trampled upon and reduced to positions of servitude and are being sacrificed worldwide. The principles of religion are uttered or utilized when or where self-servingly useful. It's becoming increasingly obvious the nations of the world today are of little faith in God or righteous principles. I've often wondered why humanity has deteriorated to the point of selfishness and immorality. Truthfully, the nations of the world today have so little compassion or consideration for fellow humans or the very environment that sustains life that it's baffling. Thus, it's not inconceivable to see how this sad state of affairs plots a course of doom. I have pondered these issues and concluded that the majority of people while ostentatiously religious have become spiritually detached.

America proclaims herself as the world leader. If this is true, she inadvertently lays claim to the world's deteriorating state. I think it's time we stop gloating over ourselves and realize our infirmities nationally. Categorically, all claims of greatness are in drastic decline in America. Normally, Americans are proud of their lifestyle, but our present condition has tarnished the pride of Americans.

Some in government crave imperialism while they're incapable of the provisional governance of America. To our national leaders equally as arrogant and defiant to righteous principles, I beg your indulgence. Words of truth are looming amid America's horizon. While we may not put stock in biblical prophecy, our present state of affairs seems to be in stark contrast with prophecy. When considered, prophecy forewarns humanity (from the books of the Apocrypha).

2 Esdras 16

They that occupy their merchandise with robbery, the more they deck their cities, their houses, their possessions, and their own persons; The more I will be angry with them for their sins, saith the Lord: Like as a whore envieth a right honest and virtuous women: So shall righteousness hate iniquity, when she decketh herself, and shall accuse her to her face, when he cometh that shall defend him that diligently searcheth out every sin upon the earth. And therefore be ye not like thereunto, nor to the works thereof.

Proportionally, Americans live lavishly seductive lives. Nevertheless, it's a grim reality that the early stages of present-day successes were ill-nourished from slavery to corruption, thievery, and the misrepresentation of righteous principles. America has made great strides through proportionally her ill-gotten gains. In my humble opinion, these practices were psychologically self-penetrating, inducing moral deficiencies. One could argue my unprofessional psychoanalysis. This, however, leaves another option. We could consider the character of the Founding Fathers or the preceding immigrants expelled from their homeland. Having said this, my point is, America and the world could be better served with a more sincere approach to spiritual principals.

To a near desperate American public, I submit that it's time we swallow our pride and present a rational display of alarm to the personal assaults, economical and otherwise, by corporate elites and government. To the majority of Americans, it's obvious everything we hold dear is under threat, lost, or out of reach. This sad commentary unfortunately further illuminates our national dilemma. Outside our borders, the opposing forces, competitors, and frenemies (supposed friends) alike are licking their chops, patiently awaiting the opportunity to further exploit America's infirmities. Once again, I appeal to the public. If ever there is a time to unite and restructure, it's now. Be advised, America. Time is of the essence.

CHAPTER 5

Greed and Poverty

Capitalism and democracy when poorly regulated promotes greed and plunge millions into poverty. My purpose in this chapter is to illuminate comprehensively the hostile and demoralizing effects of capitalism and democracy at large. Looking beyond the beguiling lifestyle of the American society warped by social economic disparities and unbounded freedoms, the reality is grim. Such grim realities illuminate the negative characteristics of capitalism: greed, selfishness, insensitivity, and moral depravity. These negative characteristics of capitalism proliferate a vicious cycle of crime, poverty, imprisonment, and wrongful death.

Indulge me while I elaborate further, giving my perspective of the woeful calamities of capitalism and democracy. America, gifted with an abundance of ingenious and intellectually renowned people, have served to her credit historically. In life, people of renowned personalities have had a profound effect in our prosperity at home and abroad. While our achievements and, proportionally, our values have sustained humanity, America's promise is in decline, and it's for these reasons that I pose this question: "What ails you, America?"

Our present state is so grave that it's become a challenge for the public to vote with any real confidence for leadership. The George W. Bush administration made bogus claims of a vibrant economy while borrowing from China. "What say you America (CNN "Out in the Open" 10/5/07)?"

It's ironic when we see the same system that made us prosperous is now failing us. While going forward in this chapter, I will endeavor to make plain the faults of our decline. If at all possible, I will do my best to avoid boring you with statistics of the cause and effect of our decline. I'll give you the benefit of the doubt that you are aware to some extent of why America is on the decline. What you may not know is the part you or I play in it. In an effort to be brief but to the point, our problems derive from an elaborate state of governmental malfeasance, greed, and an unfair distribution of wealth nationally. The short version of this decline is the mismanagement of social economics.

In today's world, a sign of good management in economics regarding the economy would be to produce a balanced budget. For the fiscal year's economic process, this would prove true to the game. However, the mismanagement at the root of our decline goes a lot deeper than an unbalanced budget. While I am not an economist, I'll try my hand at determining definitively the fiscal woes and decline of our national status. With the public as the judge of my views, we will be exercising the full weight of our democratic process for a change. While we may produce a balanced budget for the fiscal year, corporate greed, unconventional means, poverty, and insufficient funding of national support services has caused a decline.

Indulge me while I give a more in-depth illustration of the inherent infirmity that has induced our economic decline. Over time, America has succeeded in establishing a thriving economy through proportionably good work ethics. Ordinarily, a thriving economy with a balanced budget as a premise would equal success of the economy. Unfortunately, America has been plagued with crime, greed, and the underfunding of accounts necessary to sustain economic stability or productivity. While some of our ranked intellectuals may disregard my views, in this case, truth supersedes economic wizardry.

The inordinate desires of corporations and other business entities are most often accommodated by governmental leaders succumbing to the ingratiating solicitations of lobbyists. This practice, in my view, is chief among our faults for economic woes. It's my opinion that the insatiable greed of corporate elites and the apparent elitist oligarchy comprised of some in government surreptitiously manipulate a lion's portion of our cash flow, initiating our economic imbalance nationally. The American public is being hijacked, hoodwinked, and preyed upon by a form of the new-world Robin Hood. Today's Robin Hood steals from the poor and gives to the rich. While withholding the identity of the culprits of this dastardly crime, I'm confident you'll pick up.

Our government allows the outsourcing of our jobs and businesses to support the insatiable greed and expanding markets of big businesses. The government's response to our outrage was, "It's good for America." We, the American people, have had to endure massive hits financially from corporate villains and the like. With escalating crises in America, the public is still reeling from Enron, the S&L scandal, the dissipated millions in Iraq, and the list goes on.

The American consumers are being ripped off from all sides with no chance of recouping losses. We buy a house and find our scheming mortgage lenders have set us up. The housing markets are experiencing a run on foreclosures that has reaped havoc on the economy. While our government claimed progress in Iraq, the US consumers were being brutally victimized by the drastic effects of fluctuating gas hikes. Any product transferred that required gas for delivery, the company transferred the extra cost onto the consumers. Obviously, this meant well over 50 percent of all consumable goods soared in cost to consumers.

All the aforementioned negative effects to consumers are most disheartening and stressful. We, the consumers, have no recourse, and without health care, we dare not get sick. Getting sick in America has proven to be one of the most costly events in any household today. The cost of hospitalization can easily deplete life's savings and, in some cases, cost you your home and retirement plans. While hospitalization cost is financially devastating, the extended cost for aftercare can be mind boggling. While the consumers are trampled and preyed upon, our hardships seem to be beneath the radar of government. Has America lost all understanding of the responsibilities of government? It would seem so. Some members of government appear most willing to invest financially for war and proportionally environmental devastation by the elements. I say proportionally because Katrina didn't seem to meet the standards obviously necessary for critical-needs response and services.

As the woes of the public soars, so, too, does crime, imprisonment, wrongful death, and poverty. It is astoundingly perplexing when we see our political leaders educated and living comfortable lives but most unwilling to provide health care and critical needs resources for fellow citizens. To our government, I submit that greed and insensitivity with a measure of elitism will not suffice to sustain a nation. I don't propose to have all the answers; however, it's an elementary deduction to know a nation requires a constant sense of fortifying nurturance. When we listen to some of our leaders, they talk of a decline in the economy and cutting taxes at the same time. This doesn't seem rational. If your employer's pay doesn't suffice, you don't quit to do better. Furthermore, if we can't provide for the American citizenry, you don't open the floodgates for migrants, no offense to the immigrants.

It seems the melting pot societal concept wasn't well thought out. Not only is it another financial drain but it has also induced social unrest. America, even in the midst of peril, you are the greatest among nations in the world today. Despite our greatness, prudence dictates that we be wise. Surely we note that great nations are often destroyed from within. America's arrogance and insensitivity are an infirmity of character. This infirmity and the current escalation of elitism and public neglect have induced economic peril nationally. Personally, I fear a continuance on this path will be America's undoing.

As previously stated, America is currently indebted for trillions of dollars. With all due respect to the office of the president, this is madness. I don't consider myself a member of a political party for reasons of choice. Furthermore, I am not impressed with either party but quite often more disappointed with the Republican leadership. The politicians and elite supporters of the Republican Party, it appears, are for the most part wealthy and in a state of ecstasy. The Republican politicians advocate such conservatism and measure in regards to the economic crises and the public's well-being. They, however, seem to lose sight of their principles in matters of self-interest, big business, and matters unrelated to the public's critical needs. Through the use of their self-serving views, some have amassed great wealth. Unfortunately, they move at a snail's pace in their efforts to provide for critical needs, fuel resources, and the prevention of environmental pollutants.

As for the Democrats, they display more compassion and willingness to address the critical needs of the nation. It's not my intent to offend; however, they come off as passive in their approach. To me, a democracy provides optional choices and a need for public insight and involvement for success. In a personal effort of countering the realities of my criticism, I will elaborate briefly on my perspective for going forward nationally.

To the Future Leaders of the United States of America

In the leadership capacity of America, one has to concede that an unfair distribution of wealth induces economic decline and stagnates public resources. America must concede the widening gap between the rich and poor as counterproductive. The basic principle of business is supply and demand, and in business, demand is essentially the consumer. Obviously, without a demand base, there is no need for suppliers. Governmental leaders must vigorously impress upon corporate and other business leaders the deteriorating status of the American economy. The destruction of the American consumer base, in my view, is having a domino effect on American economic capabilities globally.

Despite American leaders' unwillingness to acknowledge or come clean with the public, America is in economic peril. Future presidents must assemble a crack team of the most astute professionals of renowned stature for governmental efficiency to redeem our national status. As a democratic nation, the public has to display a sense of alarm by way of the democratic process when we're troubled. Subjacent to my aforementioned perspective, there is an even greater health hazard that threatens the world. Metaphorically speaking, America is ailing. Recently, Vice President Al Gore was awarded the Nobel Peace Prize for his astute principles effectively being an alarmist to the widening of environmental hazards. I think it would be to the credit of any future president to include such a man or his insight to their administration.

Failure to establish a team to lead world efforts to prevent further environmental destruction renders efforts for the sustainment of humanity to be counterproductive at the very least. Is America to be or not to be? This becomes the question Americans must ponder as it has been, in part, your fault as citizens in our failure to boldly display alarm appropriately. Today, we have the option of choosing a path of change or inevitable self-destruction. Our present course of aggression, insatiable greed, arrogance, and imperialism is a precursor for the latter. On the other hand, if we employ prudence, change becomes the inevitable choice. While this may seem simplistic, doing right has proven to be most difficult. In effect, prudence would require America to take a hard look at herself.

This, however, would require a mirror of conscience, one that honestly reflects our principles or the lack thereof. Whatever the case, the American people must rise to the occasion. This presents an obvious challenge for a capitalistic democracy run amok. America would have to reassess her values and, in essence, putting prudent initiatives before vices and insatiable greed. Ironically, this could require the tenacious pursuit of American elitists to redirect their self-serving enterprises to be more accommodating of national interests. This could ultimately forge a more civil alliance of the American citizenry.

It has been said that in unity, there is strength. Today, it is a lack of unity that rips the very fabric of America. Indulge me as I elaborate further. Before going forward in our efforts of national resurgence or mending of international relations, we must be circumspect. In my view, America's been well-served with a new face, one that encompassed character, trust, enthusiasm, and poise. The office of the president should reflect the charisma and the overall image of America. With our economy and national status in decline, America should choose wisely for presidential leadership as it is paramount to our national interests worldwide.

The question "Is America ready for a black president?" no longer looms over America. In the face of the status quo, we had to consider all options as America is drifting into a state of chaos and anarchy. The choice of race was a luxury that was no longer rational, if ever it were. America needed to seriously support Barrack Obama as president, and did so. In my personal opinion, President Obama is what should be construed as the total package. To his credit, he is a personable person with character, enthusiasm, and poise and is most likely to be trusted internationally. He's a whole man. That effect includes the balance of a wife of esteemed character, which I believe solidifies the base of a man. President Obama is astute, God-fearing, and had an excellent grasp of what was at stake for America beyond having been fortified for the presidency.

I was certain Mr. and Mrs. Obama were acutely aware of the extenuating ramifications of such an 1003opportunity for black Americans. Having modestly illuminated their credits, their deeds have1004 determined their presidential legacy. Display alarm as needed, America, to the vanity, arrogance, and the negative aspirations of our leaders, for our future lies in the balance.

CHAPTER 6

Dictatorial Arrogance

Dictatorial arrogance is the ill-conceived pride and arrogance of the often power-crazed minds. Dictators are often psychoactively obsessed with insatiable desire, discontentment, and an emboldened ego. The arrogant dictatorial process is most often displayed in a domineering form of superiority. Imperialist nations of the past were often led by arrogant dictators in the pursuit of imperialism. Rome, Babylon, and Egypt all had arrogant dictators displaying imperialistic character to their respective societies.

History often reflects these societies or, more often, the leaders of imperialist nations to be deceived with delusions of spiritually gifted superiority. One of the great imperialists of the past, Alexander the Great, prided himself as being a god and, over time, imposing his will as such. Arrogant dictators of the past and present are similar in their pursuit of imperial status. Such nations as Hitler's Germany and Emperor Hirohito's Japan were both arrogant dictatorships that effectuated or pursued imperialism predominantly through military might and charismatic egoism. America today is perceived by some to be an arrogant dictatorial nation with domineering aspirations of imperialism. America employs a more subtle approach that is no less dictatorial, arrogant, and domineering to surrounding and distant nations.

For America, the appearance of arrogant dictatorial designs in pursuit of imperialism threatens grave consequences nationally and, thus, internationally as well. Obviously, the stakes are much higher with this being the nuclear age. When looking at the bigger picture, America is the world leader in economic turmoil, exercising poor judgment militarily and bad politics at home and abroad. Our dual-party government is a disaster and dangerously dysfunctional. Today, the American public is under siege by fellow citizens in corporate leadership and, proportionally, in government. Again, it is not my intention to exploit public fears but to awaken our seemingly naive government and to elicit a sense of alarm in the mass public.

As I labor to convey the personal fears of mine and others, some in corporate America have unleashed a more aggressive attack on the so-called middle-class consumer base in America. While the media focuses primarily on the middle class, the poor folks are literally famished by their inability to afford the bare necessities that sustain life. The poorest citizens have become so bewildered. To some, it seems futile to hope for something better. While the religious community urges the poor to keep the faith, families share apartments, poorly heated homes, homelessness, inadequate food supplies, or worse. The aforementioned events respectively to America are in fact the end results of imperialist nations historically. While America's imperialist endeavors are effectuated and categorized by way of a republic, the end results of imperialist nations are by and large indicative of the current socioeconomic events of calamitous proportion in America today.

CHAPTER 7

W.E.B. Du Bois on Capitalism

In an unforeseen intellectual linkage of perspective on capitalism, I've noted one of America's foremost intellectuals. For the record, this would be none other than the late albeit highly esteemed academic road scholar/intellectual Dr. W.E.B. Du Bois. Let it be clear to all that as the author of this book, the mere mentioning of an intellectual linkage should not be misconstrued as an implication of academic similarity. Put simply, this chapter is in essence a self-constructed collaboration of perspectives. Dr. Du Bois was born at a time in America when the intellectual genius of black folks wasn't readily embraced or openly acknowledged. With that said, I've taken this opportunity to shamelessly gloat in the afterglow of Dr. Du Bois's intellectual superiority and the manifestation of his foresight prophetically present today.

In this collaboration of perspectives and indeed in synthesis with Dr. Du Bois, I'm serving notice on capitalism in unique but no uncertain terms. As the author of this book, I've labored to illuminate the hostile effects of capitalism. Furthermore, I've articulated the negative characteristics, moral depravity, and the daunting proliferation of a vicious cycle of crime, poverty, imprisonment, and wrongful death induced by capitalism. In the American government, the Republican leadership predominately advocates a capitalist venture of free enterprise. A free enterprise system with more relaxed regulatory policies, they argue, would empower private business. Such a system offers the promise of national prosperity through a maze of trickle down theories and voodoo economics.

Dr. Du Bois, in addition to a billowing surge of intellectual capital, had a long and diversified academic career, teaching subjects ranging from Greek and Latin to sociology, history, and economics. Dr. Du Bois argued credibly to date that private ownership and free enterprise were leading the world down a slippery slope. My words, not his.

Dr. Du Bois once, in speaking public, stated (paraphrasing) that it had taken him some time to reach a conclusion regarding capitalism but that after careful deliberation, he concluded capitalism can't reform itself. It was his opinion that capitalism was doomed to self-destruction and that no system of universal selfishness could bring social good to all (see W.E.B. Du Bois's book *Of Our Spiritual Strivings*).

Today, the leading nations of the world persist respectively to their self-serving perspectives of sociology. But what have we here? While America clings to opposing exploits of capitalism in contrast with elements of socialism economically, ironically, world economies are collectively intertwined. With America ostensibly at the helm of world economies, socioeconomically, the world has been drawn into a predominately capitalist enterprise. If the events of today regarding the economy are indeed a prelude to tomorrow; it would seem Dr. Du Bois's perspective on capitalism has peaked in credibility. In effect, capitalism has failed to provide a fair distribution of wealth. As a result, capitalism has caused America to collapse from a three-tier to a two-tier economic society.

Black America salutes Dr. W.E.B. Du Bois for his tireless intellectual contributions to us as a people: "Wisdom never dies, knowledge is endless and understanding prevails."

CHAPTER 8

Anarchy

Once upon a time in the West, America was the torch that illuminated the path of prosperity. America of late has sought to intertwine capitalism with a measure of socialism.

In effect, capitalism is being transmuted in principle in a futile attempt to suffice the insatiable greed of the elite. Socialism, a term and practice in conjunction with capitalism, provides a tactical method to circumvent fairness in the efforts to proliferate elitism. Today, capitalism is most applicable and beneficial for the elite. While socialist exploits are used to suppress wages and benefits, the quality of life for the American people is suppressed. It's by the use of such tactical exploits in big businesses that wages are stagnated—the rich get richer, ultimately reclassifying the working class as the working poor. As a result, our economic system has evolved from a selfish exploit to a self-destructive escapade of unconscionable greed. If my observations seem excessive, consider the cost of living and America's unconscionable business pursuits of cheap labor and the like.

In my opinion, it's by the obsessive compulsion induced by capitalism that corporate power brokers of big business entities are driven to insatiable greed, thievery, recklessness, and environmental destruction. The trifling perpetrators of the recent mortgage crises, obviously immoral and unprincipled, have wrecked havoc on the national economy and abroad. Thus, it is today a well-known fact that power corrupts.

Power, by its corruptive effects, often induces the inadvertent corruption of the well-meaning of today's society. For the record, when I speak of power, I'm speaking predominately of the societal elite effectuating elitist designs and, in effect, plutocrats possessed by capitalism's obsessive tendencies.

The lives of the American people are stagnated and overwhelmed by the harsh realities and physical effects of the rising cost of living. In the wake of the housing crises, millions have lost their jobs, houses, health care, and what had become a civil way of life. It doesn't take a psychologist to tell you that the deterioration of your civil life and the loss of family and stability over time induces stress, desperate conditions, and desperate measures.

America, a country gifted with innovative technology and an accomplished academia, is now shamefully adrift, aimless. Once again, I ask, what ails you, America? With all your greatness, you're troubled. With your ostensibly vast spectrum of wealth and opportunity, the public is suffering calamitously. In America today, democracies waning as crime is rampant, the economy is stagnant, and like me, an untold number of citizens are homeless. The American people shocked and dismayed are beginning to experience the manifold extremities of poverty.

America is presently facing bankruptcy in predominately every state and local government with the dissipating chants of greatness still echoing in the halls of the elite. Stunningly, the obtuse and obstinate minds of some in government are incapable of appreciating the severity of our plight. Thus, I'm compelled to ask, how does America define her greatness today? Do we simply compare ourselves to some of our barbarous foes or third world countries? How do we justify our claims of greatness? With health care, education, gainful employment, and the

American dream out of reach, unattainable, or prevented via social stratification, the American way of life is waning. Anarchy is in the wind. With sedition, insurgency, and insurrection on the rise, anarchy's on the horizon.

Capitalism is today for the benefit of America's wealthy elite. It's the top 1 percent of the American society that predominately owns or controls employment, wages, land, and capital goods in America. The wealthy elitists through socialist exploits are increasingly limiting society's ability to profit or to engage in competitive economic activity. In essence, capitalism is being transmuted to something more insatiably self-serving. Such conditions are ripening America for anarchy and self-destruction.

Put simply, our system of capitalism is not unlike other systems of governance today—cruel and overwhelming. Modern-day social orders exceedingly empower the elite, effectively manipulating and dominating humanity with what appears initially as palatable and life-sustaining systems. The egotistical minds of the wealthy elitists in America are compelled by the insatiable greed induced by capitalism. They are, as a result, obsessed with maintaining control of our humanistically structured way of life. The following excerpts are corroborating evidence as relatively pertinent.

Making Class Invisible
Gregory Mantsios
Readings for Sociology

(This is an excerpt from the book *Readings for Sociology* edited by Garth Massey.)

Poverty in the United States is systemic. It is a direct result of economic and political policies that deprive people of jobs, adequate wages, or legitimate support. It is neither natural nor inevitable (*Readings for Sociology*, p. 201).

The Positive Functions of Poverty
Herbert J. Gans
Readings for Sociology

The poor subsidize, directly and indirectly, many activities that benefit the affluent. For one thing, they have long supported both the consumption and investment activities of the private economy by virtue of the low wages which they receive. This was openly recognized at the beginning of the industrial revolution, When a French writer quoted by T.H. Marshall [forthcoming, p. 7] pointed out that to assure and maintain the prosperities of our industries, it is necessary that the workers should never acquire wealth. Examples of this kind of subsidization abound even today. The concept of subsidy used here, thus assumes belief in a just wage [see bottom of p. 22].

Today, it's the exalted perpetrators of capitalism's ill contrived devices that continue to infect and indeed prey upon main stream society. America has been pledged by an onslaught of calamitous events of insurance fraud, housing foreclosures and massive unemployment. It's through the socioeconomic system respectively to the unfair distribution of wealth via incomes and proportionally the designs of the elite, that wages are ill measured and citizens corrupted. A point in fact; some of America's chief administrators of leading financial institutions have been investigated for fraudulent act's relatively to the housing foreclosures. The alleged criminal acts perpetrated resulting in the housing foreclosure crises were unconscionable, indicative and synonymous with modern day carpet bagging. As the federal government scrambles to get a handle on joblessness and the housing crises; the prospective home buyers "American citizens" as a result, have been reduced to mere squatters and homelessness. While members of our political parties call for an end to government spending; they argue, it expands the deficit sinking America further into the abyss, respectively to debt.

Clearly, America's debt crises, jobs and the current war are at the height of America's periling endeavors. The current economic crises and its volatile repercussions have not only destabilized international markets; the world's "super powers" are beginning to cringe as the relentless effects of the economic crises are felt around the world. While England's government contemplated massive cuts to maintain economic stability; recently the citizens of France and Grease have taken to the streets rioting in revolt to the dismal effects of the world economic crises. The HHK world news reported "in Japan some 1.4 million households received welfare rising by 11% in 2010 sense last year". On 11/3/2010, the ABC news reported the Federal Reserve announced a bold plan to try to invigorate the economy by buying 600 billion more in treasury bonds; this, in the aftermath of the perches of some 1.7 trillion in mortgage and treasury bonds bought by the FED in 2009, all in hopes of bolstering the economy. (An excerpt by Jeannine Aversa, the AP economics writers, Nov. 3, 2010)

Even analysts who favor the FED's bond purchases cautioned against expecting them to rescue the sluggish economy. "Bottom line: The plan provides a boost to the economy's growth, but it is not going to solve our problems," said Mark Zandi, chief economist at Moody's Analytics. "Even with the FED's action, we're going to feel uncomfortable about the economy in the next six to twelve months."

Politicians, world leaders, and indeed some of the most profound economists have unleashed a maze of discombobulating conjecture geared for solutions to the world's economic crises. In this aggressive campaign of ostensibly the world's intellectual elite and economic gurus, they endeavor to circumvent the inevitability of karma. If in reality the end justifies the means, we have to conceder karma as part of our socioeconomic equation as it is most indicative of just weights and balances. Why karma, you ask. Socioeconomics effect or affect human behavior and the vast spectrum of societal life respective to how economic principles are effectuated socially.

When there's an unfair distribution of wealth, adverse conditions are induced socially. In my humble opinion, America has historically dealt unfairly with its public, some more than others. After at least a century of free labor, selectively suppressed wages, and the cunning manipulation and capitalization of the precious endowments of slaves and their descendants, America has amassed the greatest empire of the modern-day era.

While there are those who would argue karma has no bearing on socioeconomic effects, I respectfully disagree. Karma is in essence a vengeful result and reflection of God's heated displeasure with the ill deeds of humanity. The hand of God effectuates justice as it is indelibly involved in all the events of life. Indeed, it is the Lord who balances by his will the scales of justice in the balances of life. The following is a stunning revelation of sorts illuminated by one of the most profound intellectuals of the modern-day era respectively to karma conceptually as I perceive it.

Of Rogues and Geldings
Barbara J. Fields
Historian Extraordinaire

From the *American Historical Review*, the following excerpts are relevant as they relate idealistically to the invariable albeit spiritually predisposed notion of karma.

Barbara J. Fields illuminates: "Thomas Jefferson's notes, 163. Lewis P. Simpson argues that query XVIII marks a crisis in Jefferson's faith in the capacity of reason to solve the problems of human society and human history; see 'Land, slaves, and mind, 25–28.'"

> Indeed I tremble for my country when I reflect that God is just: that his justice cannot sleep for ever: that considering numbers, nature and natural means only, a revolution of the wheel of fortune, an exchange of situation, is among possible events: that it may

become probable by supernatural interference! (Thomas Jefferson)

The aforementioned excerpts are relevant in that they illustrate what I've interpreted as karma being contemplated by Thomas Jefferson respective to slavery in America. While otherwise artfully articulated by Thomas Jefferson, he consciously considered the possibility and indeed the probability of karma (i.e., God's justice) relative to slavery. Furthermore, it should be duly noted that slavery was at that time a critical component of American economic mobility. Obviously, blatant slavery doesn't exist today, having been refined or recycled by the obscuring stratagem of the assimilation of slaves by America and others.

Today, it's the euphemism of the late Barbara J. Fields, a noted intellectual, for slavery and race/racism that conveys its demeaning and substandard ill effects socially and economically. In my opinion, it was by and large the unfair distribution of wealth in the pursuit of elitism and ultimately racism born out of the insane craze for elitism that had culminated America's economic imbalance, thus resulting in the resent collapse of the economy. Ironically, it's the socioeconomic structure built upon the ill-contrived notions of capitalism's faulty philosophical premise that may indeed, at long last, prove Dr. Du Bois's seemingly prophetic foresight in perspective of capitalism's calamitous demise. While I don't specialize in marketing, economics, or employment, I think it's absurd the movers and shakers of government are today essentially at a stalemate. Thus, I think it's completely irrational for politicians to block government spending while employers aren't hiring and the economy is in decline.

Today, even the distribution of unemployment insurance benefits are frowned upon, so I pose this question: What's our strategy, America? Obviously, doing more with less isn't a workable solution to today's economy as it is merely an inevitable feat for survival without promise. When we consider the history that precluded and indeed produced America and her Founding Fathers, there was a self-serving mind-set that initiated the expulsion of the Founding Fathers by their ancestors.

In my observation of life today and the historic accounts of the Founding Fathers and their ancestors, they bear a striking similarity correlative of sorts. It seems apparent there's a habitual inclination of elitism widely pervasive or inherently characteristic of some of the Caucasian people of America as their forbearers. Elitism denoted is the belief that certain persons or members of certain classes or groups deserve favored treatment by virtue of their perceived superiority as in intellect, social status, or financial resources. Capitalism and democracy's elite proponents infused with elitism and excessive freedoms make for a potent concoction that deteriorates human virtue with reckless effects socioeconomically.

CHAPTER 9

Today

With respect to employment and retirement in America, unless you're well-off, one is fast becoming as distressing as the other in America. You know, it's one thing to lose your footing or to become disenchanted, but when you begin to lose your bearing, you're becoming unglued. I know. I get it when people say, "No one said life would be easy." However, when you experience the toils or the absolute woes of life in America, the leading nation of the world, it's troubling.

Life today is, for most, a very unforgiving escapade of broken promises and very little peace of mind. In this capitalistic democracy, life has become so burdensome that even the pivotal moments of life are too costly or problematic. Take for instance marriage. It is perhaps arguably one of the most pivotal moments in the structure of life. It has ceased to be the most virtuous and affectionate intercourse of humanity but functions more like a business. Marriage today requires as much business terminology or toil as a corporate venture. Hard work and long-term planning, budgeting, contracting, savings and loans, insurance, and capital investments of sorts are all requirements for a successful marriage. With the aforementioned contingencies for new and existing families becoming increasingly difficult, the social structure of America is unraveling.

I'm beginning to wonder if a restructuring of American governance could prove more social economically sound. Today, health care and education for most are literally unaffordable, and the national and local state governments are economically in deficit. Perhaps it's time we stop boasting about our failing system of capitalism and democracy to consider our calamitous state of humanity. When we saw our schools systems were failing the students, President Obama effectuated new policies and procedures geared for resolution.

These bold new policies and procedures called for the reevaluation of the intellectual prowess of teachers and administrators and the redistribution of critical resources. When our military brass doesn't perform or suffers a loss of perspective immeasurably, invariably, they're replaced. With respect to Congress and Senate's responsibility for America's shared values, leadership, and the safeguarding of virtues, righteousness and justice are often weighed in the balances of the fluctuating strengths of political parties. It's my belief that righteousness and justice are born out of spiritual principles that when embraced, we (humans) are made responsible and beholden to God first and, thereby, humanity.

With respect to our political leaders, their responsibilities, and the periling state of the country, I think our woes to some extent reflect the divisiveness and often fluctuating ill-contrived ideals of our politicians. Surely I'd be remiss were I not to mention our wealthy elite in this nexus of self-destruction unfolding in America. The American elitist business matrix, metaphorically speaking, functionally s indicative of a colonized conglomerate of predator drones. Predominately, corporate elites in our capitalist business matrix categorically hone in on the vulnerable, wreaking havoc and destruction, in particular like the housing foreclosure crises or worst. Nevertheless, America's capitalist democracy has been the envy of the world and the gateway to the advancement of modern-day civilization. Today, America is faltering. Presently, America is effectuating the most catastrophic calamities ever to affect world nations collectively.

America's system of capitalism and democracy, embraced like the gift that keeps on giving, is now stalling and wreaking havoc on the world's economy. This is, in my view, a pivotal state in time to respective power brokers, and quite possibly a game changer. Today, American politicians and corporate elites are in a race to place the blame for the dismal state of the economy at the feet of anyone but themselves. When Ronald Reagan was the president, he effectuated the unsuccessful policies of trickle-down economics. The succeeding president George Bush Sr., it appears, was content with the preceding policies of Reaganomics, sufficing his political/economic ideologies. Thus, he acquiesced.

President Bill Clinton responded to the periling effects of Reaganomics nationally. In an extraordinary feat of political and economic savvy, he balanced the budget while bolstering the economy, leaving a hefty surplus. While there are those who salute his successor, President George W. Bush, for the ousting of the barbarous Saddam Hussein, we were troubled, to say the least, by his endgame. President George W. Bush was predominately perceived by mainstream society to have literally squandered a $127 billion surplus inherited from the Clinton administration.

Few, if any, presidents in American history have been so well-accommodated for success from the premise of a balanced budget coupled with an economic surplus as the former President George W. Bush. While this president was equipped, in my opinion, to exceed his predecessors, it seems he did the least for many and the most for the few. It's this president who vigorously effectuated policies to accommodate big business in shipping jobs overseas while telling the American public it was good for America. So once again, it's for the possessive-obsessive tendencies of capitalism and the sure bliss of ignorance that we should be thankful today, I guess. Thus, I'm compelled to ask, was it also America's goal in her race to the top to increasingly become a borrower more so than a nurturer? How is the wisdom of America sought out?

America—in her nexus of elitism, pride, and principles as boastfully characterized quite liberally realistically it seems— is becoming even more empathetically and compassionately obscured. Our government recently elected to further extend our strained military resources in Libya in an effort to stave off the mounting deaths of the Libyan people as a result of their troubled affairs. After some forty years of Muammar al-Gaddafi's rule in Libya, the United States president Obama, being politically correct, arguably, has chosen amid repeated requests to intervene. President Obama, poised with due caution yet sympathetic, contends it was a matter of principle and humanitarianism as I understand him. While America secretly prides herself as an empire nationally, as a nation, America has to be true to herself.

America is a periling nation literally on foreign life support. I think it incumbent on the American people to abandon foolish pride and to effectuate more appropriately status-based principles! Granted, it's a well-known fact America has been the most appreciative and accommodating of global plight humanitarianly, nevertheless, our humanitarian efforts while morally and humanely courageous in view of our present circumstances, our compassion is quite often displaced.

In a presidential address to the American public, President Obama made it a point to expound briefly on his reason/justification for his intervening in Libya. In this address, he talked about the difference between America, China, and other leading nations respective to why America reacts differently to global plight. In a brief summary, the president stated that America is different in that America acts out of long-standing traditions respective to characteristics and principles. While I understand and accept the president's views on this issue, absent some unknown factors, I'll state for the record to reiterate that I disagree with him on principle and timing for such humanitarian endeavors.

With reports of the same levels of violent unrest in Syria by A.B.C. News on April 25, 2011, this poses a question: What now? Principally, I would urge President Obama to remain conscious of the fact that he's a uniquely different president at a pivotal state in time. I would remind the president that America today is not the America of yesterday. Furthermore, you can't do the same things and expect something different. I'd state for the record, Mr. President, it's the characteristics and principles of yesterday that got America in the grave condition it is in today. It's my opinion that if America is to survive going forward, she will have to engage her future endeavors with a progressively different sense of selfishness. Ironically, it's a form of selfishness I'd contend the American people had hoped for when voting for President Obama. It's the type of selfishness that in effect puts the critical needs of the American people appropriately ahead of elitism, imperialist designs, and humanitarian efforts abroad.

Beyond my aforementioned perspective, it should be clear to all that the voters voted for President Obama out of their personal appreciation for his intellectual prowess conveyed by his superb oratory and bona fide credentials. There's an underline fear growing increasingly evident every day in America—that is, the governmental party's dissention has become insurmountable. America, it's time we're true to ourselves. A black man doesn't just waltz into Iowa or New Hampshire and obtain the delegates necessary for the presidency, qualified or not. Having said this, I think it's time we come clean.

In the aftermath of the George W. Bush administration, America was troubled and in need of astute leadership, racial pedigree notwithstanding. It's been said a drowning man will grab a straw, and a condition will make you change. In essence, our desperate condition requires competence and a strategically balanced approach. When the president was embraced and indeed voted for across racial lines, I think to a great extent it was a result of our dismal state nationally and the urgent need for greater intellectualism in the presidency. Nevertheless, it's my opinion that with the public having elected President Obama and later empowering a Republican-led Congress, this was a recipe for gridlock.

In recognition of the aforementioned facts respectively to a black president, I think it should be viewed by Black Americans as skeptically measured growth in America. Why skeptically measured, you ask. I think it's wise that we guard against becoming overly optimistic as optimism is a generic virtue that's quite often misleading. For Black America, complacency and optimism are in effect the pitfalls for those well-adjusted to the status quo in America, hence the question posed by the esteemed Dr. Cornel West: "What are we well-adjusted to?" Is it our rapidly deteriorating plight respective to joblessness, incarcerations, poor health care, and homelessness? Is it the scandalous exploitation and character assassination of one of our most gifted black artists as illuminated by Minister Farrakhan, respective to the great Michael Jackson? Once again, what are we well-adjusted to?

I would argue that in this capitalistic democracy, it's the often biased, sociologically contrived stratagems that produced the Emancipation Proclamation that perpetuates proportionally the delusion of blacks. This delusion appropriately framed as an illusion was expounded upon and contextualized as the illusion of inclusion by the esteemed Dr. Julia Hare. With respect to her intellectualism, Julia Hare lays the game down with no uncertain terms. With the flavor of the hood and an all-black perspective, her blackness is beautiful as she gives America the business (see The State of the Black Union 2007 on YouTube).

Let's face it; it's the aforementioned stratagem of subjugation that effectuated our assimilation and the unconventional frame of life that is African Americanism. For the record, it's the same perplexing mind-set that conceived the psychological, predatory-inducing system of capitalism, slavery, and elitism that now perpetuates racism. In the end, I think it's humanity's unwillingness to conform to the righteous orientation that is in effect the will of the Lord. While humanity has succeeded in producing what could only be construed as a state of worldwide surrealism respective to the manifold courses of life, it's the catastrophically insurmountable will of the Lord that will ultimately be exalted as with world nations of the past.

With America at the helm of the world, foreign nations are literally being seduced by America's grandiose allure of democracy. Today, the Arab nations of the Middle East are literally following suit in waves of insurrection arguably in pursuit of democracy. Not long ago, Americans fought among themselves while enslaving African Americans in the construction of America's democracy. Today, the Arabs are being slaughtered by their own governments in an obscuring quest of opposing views on democracy. What is it about the social order of humanity that breeds dissention, death, and destruction?

While it's obvious America's democracy is not the solution to the predominate ills of humanity, it has proven to be the most palatable for the modern-day era. With that said, it appears all social orders in the world theater today, as sociologically sustainable systems for humanity and the ecosystem at large; they're all failing.

Democracy, communism, autocracy, and socialism are all opposing doctrines of humanistic ally structured social orders. Metaphorically speaking, human beings are like machines. While we're catastrophically superior to machines, like machines, it's the creator's operations manual (i.e., the Ten Commandments) that provides for maximum performance. I've been blessed with a fairly palpable appreciation for God's work respective to humanity and the world. A word to the wise would be that humanity reverts to the spiritually inspired doctrines of the Old Testament Bible for the premise of sociological reorientation.

America's system of capitalism and democracy has led the world with respect to productivity and a sociologically palatable facet of life. Life in America, while sociologically palatable, is perceived predominately by blacks and our intellectuals to be intrinsically ostentatious. America quite often speaks with ambiguity or ambivalence, promising one thing but delivering another, thereby illusionary at best. America is today on an unsustainable path of debt induced by the unconscionable greed indicative of the possessive tendencies of capitalism. It's for the aforementioned reasons I urge the public to display alarm to what are in fact the hostile effects of capitalism and democracy. To quote Mr. Jeff Faux of the Economic Policy Institute, "With American elitist's designs for full scale globalization; world economic and business elites are poised to dominate markets, unrestrained by ill equipped regulatory policies and or necessary institutions for global expansion."

When considering the effects of the overall ramifications of the aforementioned endeavors in depth, Jeff Faux concludes, "Democracy is rendered futile," and I agree. The aforementioned practice lends credence to my perspectives on the hostile effects of capitalism and democracy. While I can't be construed as a credible source for a professional perspective on economics globally, I direct your attention to more of the astute perspectives of Mr. Jeff Faux of the Economic Policy Institute (see *The Global Class War* by Jeff Faux).

When observing life in America, I'm inclined to ask, where are the minds of our academic administrators? Today, the price of a college education has skyrocketed to the tune of some one hundred forty thousand dollars variably. One would expect college teachers and administrators to be grievously alarmed at such an obvious threat to their careers. With the economy in the sack and unemployment hovering at 9 percent as of May 06, 2011, college students have begun rallying in protest of the escalating cost of tuitions. President Obama, in his optimistic view for the future, talks of America's need to advance in education and technology if we are to continue as leaders of the free world (my words, not his). Clearly, the American citizenry will have to forge a united front to combat the insatiable greed of the elitist oligarchy and proponents of unbridled capitalism in this democracy.

Today, our governing elites continue to clamor over the right path for entitlements, health care, and the like. In the *Chicago Sun-Times* news report dated May 23, 2011, it states that "the number of emergency rooms in rural areas in the US fell 27 percent between 1990 and 2009, according to a study published the prior week in the journal of the American Medical Association. That's an average of 89 closures per year according to the A.M.A. report. The loss of emergency rooms nationwide since 1990 is a concern because ER visits have increased 35 percent since then, said Renee Hsia, author of the new study." As I continue to observe the calamitous dilemmas besetting America, I'm simply baffled by some of our government and business leaders' unwillingness to concede the obvious. When logically assessed, it's the critically imbalanced distribution of wealth and the insatiable greed of the elite that expands and perpetuates our socioeconomic woes nationally.

Indicative of the aforementioned logic, America continues to spend billions upon billions on the expanding war, the futile attempts at nation building overseas, and the escalating cost of homeland security. In today's obscuring wars to defend the American way of life, a way of life increasingly becoming more daunting than the ill effects of the war itself, Americans are perplexed. Arguably, it's the hostile effects of capitalism's obsessive tendencies, the war, and an often-biased democracy ingrained with elitism that plagues America. With extraordinary deficits in parallel nationally, the American people are being constrained socioeconomically in every respect.

The ill effects of the economic crises are beginning to take a more daunting effect beyond the socioeconomic aspects of life. It seems there's an ominous change occurring publically. People appear weary, impatient, and at times unabashedly cantankerous. In what I perceive as a traumatic change in people albeit psychologically, the unique variances notwithstanding with respect to cause and effect, I surmise the changes to have been induced by the economic crises. When observing people in person or through the media, it's clear families are suffering in their efforts to make ends meet. The severely disoriented and often the most impoverished youths are becoming more hostile as criminal flash mobs, street hustlers, and socially indignant, estranged, and misguided youths.

When observing the bitterly disenfranchised, the grim realities of poverty and despair are beginning to come to light as prosperity sinks into the abyss submerged by waves of unemployment spun by the insatiable greed of the elite. The foreclosed homes and closed businesses aligned on neighborhood streets have become petrified monuments, a testament to the turning of the tide from prosperity to sure calamity. The remaining small business proprietors economically beleaguered stand anxiously in the doorways of their respective shops and businesses while desperately gawking down the once bustling streets of commercial districts. Our schoolteachers, medical facilitators, and the public at large are being bombarded by the complexities of an increasingly hostile and socioeconomically perplexed society.

Currently, teachers are being judged or held responsible for failing to meet the obscuring expectations of educating the disenfranchised and otherwise ailing students. Students who are often times socially malnourished, unconventionally bred, impoverished, and frustrated are by and large restrained by the rising cost associated with the necessary accommodations for life and school. The aforementioned conditions complicate and exasperate the educational process for students and teachers alike. In America, it seems the predominate power brokers of government and businesses are driven and misguided by capitalist designs to sustain an elitist oligarchy. With nationalism notwithstanding, the pillars of American greatness are buckling with seasoned intellectuals looking on. The academic administrators and governing officials are discombobulated or perplexed at the very least.

Having severely crippled the terrorist networks, President Obama initiated the winding down of what had seemed to be an endless military campaign. Today, the awesome task of rebuilding America takes center stage. America, literally a nation in peril and with the economy and academic institutions in crises, the future is precarious at best. Our politicians bicker tirelessly, ranting about their seemingly ostentatious concerns for America's future. While it's often said our children are the future, without economic and academic resources in place, the grim realities of today offer very little promise for the future.

While the American people continue to struggle with the effects of the recent recession and 2013 sequester, empathy seems a rare virtue in the halls of Congress as American officials endeavor to make the largest cuts to entitlement programs in American history. Predominately, the American people until recently lived their lives taking much for granted. For the American citizens, the vast spectrum of a humanistically devised civilization and the surrealism of modernization has grown to be commonplace realities in the lives of the American public. To America's credit, she has succeeded in the manifestation of what I perceive as extended variations of surrealism respective to the imagination as revealed in dreams or otherwise subconsciously. Through the vast opportunities and near unbridled freedoms of capitalism and democracy, variably, America has soared in the vanities of her dreams.

America, through her diverse resources of wit, ingenuity, and ideals, has made manifest, even surpassing the things her Founding Fathers dared to dream. Through the boldness of her imagination and often obscured principles, America has effectuated the flight of humanity, the technological modernization of mass industry, and proportionately the disorientation of humanity respective to the manifold courses of life. For America having been ostensibly embraced by pockets of the world, I pose this question: To what end? Ironically for America, it seems to be something in the framework of mortifying irony that she is plagued for her self-proclaimed greatness. America, for all your greatness albeit most obscuring, your enemies are mounting; and by those you seek to befriend, you're made leery.

In life, we find it's wise to hope for the best but to prepare for the worst. Has biblical prophecy made reference to America at this time? "O' thou that dwellest upon many waters, abundant in treasures, thine end is come, and the measure of thy covetousness" (Jeremiah 51:13). If you doubt the aforementioned prophecy, I'm compelled to ask, what's ailing you, America? At one point, America claimed to be the wealthiest nation on earth; and in conjunction with that, she's the leader of the free world. With respect to the latter statement, if this is true, it would appear the free world is in jeopardy as America faces profound crises from sea to shining sea.

In a recent press release respective to America's economic crises, President Obama urged Republican leaders to stop procrastinating, later stating (paraphrasing) that everyone must eat their peas. The president, irritated with particular party heads' unwillingness to do their jobs, became humorously sarcastic in implying perceivably to a sense of immaturity displayed by opposing party members in a critical budget meeting at the White House (see ABC News on or around July 12, 2011).

Being spiritually inclined, I would be utterly remiss were I not to interject God's omnipotence relative to world events, humanistic and otherwise. As world nations contend with the hostile effect of capitalism and democracy's economic downturn globally, it appears America and world nations are increasingly coming under siege by way of the elements—earthly upheavals and the catastrophic effects befitting the wrath of the Lord. Having studied biblically, it's my understanding the earth's environment and the atmospheric elements were formed to accommodate the sustainment of life and its perpetuation. Today, the supposed vanguards of humanity's domain and leading nations of the world are in effect the culprits of the most catastrophic destruction and pollution to the atmosphere, natural environment, and the world's ecosystem at large.

As previously stated in the introduction of this book, to have dominion over the earth is to have stewardship requiring planetary and environmental considerations effectuated through our responsibilities and deeds as humans. By virtue of the apparent disorientation of respective nations globally, humanity is becoming increasingly hostile, predatory, self-destructive, and degenerative. Verily the disorientation of nations is a result of being religiously disingenuous, thus abominably deteriorating morally and psychologically to a state of ungodliness and truculence. If, in an oblivious state of mind, you doubt the latter statement, I direct your attention to the socially deteriorating state of the American society, our gridlocked government, and humanity at large globally. Dr. Cornel West, in one of his many lectures abroad, expounded on the ill-conceived notion of a self-made man. Dr. West illuminated the fact that no man gives birth to himself or molds himself to be the man he becomes. In concurrence with Dr. West yet again, boldly I might add with awesome certainty that as there are no self-made men, the same is true for the nations of the world. It's through the preeminent will and insurmountable omnipotence of God that the manifold courses of life are predestine and effectuated. Thus, humanity at large is subject to God's righteous indignation for our deviations from the Old Testament's biblically inscribed precepts.

Previously, I spoke of world nations being under siege by the elements and thereby God. Bear with me while I elaborate briefly. As stated in the preface of this book, God puts men in power over nations, and their ill will contrary to God's will does not go unchecked by divine intervention. For a compelling illustration of the Lord's unleashing of the elements in a tumultuous assault on humanity in response to the proliferation of ill deeds, I direct your attention to biblical scriptures pertinent and solidified factually in literality.

On numerous occasions, the Lord effectuated the use of the elements in his efforts to stave off the evil deeds of man. The first known use of the elements was in the book of Genesis with a flaming sword that turned every way to keep the way of the tree of life (Genesis 3:24). As the wickedness of humanity escalated, so, too, did the wrath of the Lord and his use of the elements. As with Noah and the great flood (Genesis 7:12) and in Sodom and Gomorrah with fire and brimstone (General

19:24), the use of the elements has become a familiar pattern in the display of the Lord's heated displeasure. Today, the economic crises, tornadoes, massive flooding, hurricanes, tsunamis, drought, earthquakes, and the dissipating waterways are all in stark contrast with prophecy of today and historic accounts of the past. The relevant prophecy of today being manifested makes references to a prophecy of desolation forthcoming. (For a better understanding and pertinent interpretation of prophecy, see another of my books entitled *Praising God: The Way Home for So-called African Americans*).

When I see the devastating effects and the affrighted amazement of victims of the catastrophic effects of tornadoes and the like, I'm regretfully saddened and reminded of a biblically inscribed version of tornadoes biblically termed fanners. First and foremost, I think it's critically important that we have a better understanding of the source and reason for the punishingly catastrophic effects of the elements. Hear now the wisdom of Jeremiah the Lord's prophet. "He [God] made the earth by his power; he hath established the world by his wisdom and hath stretched out the heavens by his understanding. When he uttereth his voice, there is a multitude of waters in the heavens; and he causeth the vapors to ascend from the ends of the earth: he maketh lightnings with rain, and bringeth forth the wind out of his treasures" (Jeremiah 51:15–16).

When considering the biblically historic events of old in contrast with the current events of today, it becomes clear the disasters incurred by the elements are the work of the Lord. In the book of Jeremiah, the Lord demonstrates his omnipotent ability to summon the destructive forces of the elements at will for the destruction of his enemies. It's not a fluke of nature! "Thus saith the Lord; Behold, I will raise up against Babylon— [i.e., captivities or Gentile nations], and against them that dwell in the midst of them that rise up against me a destroying wind;

and will send unto Babylon fanners [i.e., tornadoes or hurricanes] that shell fan her, and shell empty her land: for in the day of trouble they shell be against her round about" (Jeremiah 51:1–2). Astonishingly, the irony is, the elements that were used to create and sustain life are utilized in a punishing means of destruction.

In closing, with respect to glorified ideologies like capitalism and democracy, the words of biblical psalms are looming. "The Lord is known by the judgment which he executeth: the wicked is snared in the work of his own hands" (Psalms 9:16). Case in point, the insatiable greed of the elite that induced the foreclosure crises and the like have brought America and the world economy to the brink of collapse. In my opinion, there has been very little justice for the victims of some of the most treacherous crimes perpetrated by wealthy elites against the poor.

> He that oppresseth the poor to increase his riches, and he that giveth to the rich shall surely come to want. (Proverbs 23:16)

> For the needy shall not always be forgotten: the expectation of the poor shall not perish forever. (Psalms 9:18)

> Put them in fear, O Lord: that the nations may know themselves to be but men. (Psalms 9:20)

Thus, it's for the aforementioned ill deeds and the like that world nations are today under siege by the Lord.

The End

About the Author

In the summer of 1963, my family of two parents, four sisters, and six brothers moved into the projects, aka Chicago's public housing. Unbeknownst to us at that time, in retrospect, the projects projected a subtle allure of tranquility with the potential for a pernicious transmutation socially. As a young man growing up in the projects, I was confronted with some of my greatest challenges in life. While predominately self-educated, I had to endure the pitfalls, traps, and snares of an impoverished ghetto life comprised of social and psychological indifferences induced by a scarcely cultivated environment.

It's my belief, based upon the profound wisdom and prophecies of the Old Testament Bible, that I can make a positive impact on life, expounding on the often-veiled ills of humanity. As one of the major events of my life, with the hopes of a positive effect on society, I've authored the book entitled *Be Alarmed!*

Summary: America's system of capitalism democracy is on a downhill spiral and cannot continue to go unchecked. It has presently become a vicious cycle with an influx of greed, crime, poverty, and psychological despair. Thus, I submit to concerned members of the government and society at large that we must display alarm and elicit change.